Praise for

A Real Mother

"Denise Malloy gives us a deliciously snarky, loving, and brutally honest look at REAL motherhood. Not one to pretend our little bundles of joy don't also bug the crap out of us, Denise tells it like it is. For those of us in the thick of "It" (as one tends to refer to one's child when blaming one's partner), we can know we are not alone, and if Denise is any indication, we don't have to throw out our sense of humor with the bath water."
- Katie Goodman, comedian, creator of "*Broad Comedy*," and author of *Improvisation for the Spirit*.

"In this hilarious collection where wry humor and loving warmth prevail, Denise Malloy's foray into parenthood puts her at the pinnacle with Erma Bombeck and Dave Barry. A must-read for anyone who ever laughed or cried over being a kid or a Real parent."
-Lauri Olsen, Author of *Cold Moon Honor, Whispers on the Wind*

"Denise Malloy has one of those remarkable outlooks that can turn any situation into comedy. I never miss the chance to read her column in the *Bozeman Daily Chronicle* and when I picked up her book, *A Real Mother,* I happily settled in for a good laugh. Perhaps it strikes a chord because I, too, am a MOM and every scenario that Denise pens has the tendency to sound familiar. Whether you are a mom, dad or a former kid, there is bound to be a story in this repertoire that will make you chuckle and as my Grandmother used to say, 'laughing is good for the soul.'"
-Jennifer Lowe-Anker, mother, artist and author of *Forget Me Not*

"Denise Malloy reminds readers that you don't have to be crude or edgy to be gut-bustingly funny. Call her a modern-day Erma Bombeck, but somehow she manages to consistently slice and dice modern-day living with good old-fashioned humor. While no pet or human in her family is excused from her keen eye for the absurd (and then writing about it), she perhaps shines brightest when poking fun at herself - which she does, often."
-Megan Ault Regnerus, Managing Editor, *Montana Quarterly* and *Balance Magazines,* blogger, *minor catastrophes*

a real mother

stumbling through motherhood

Denise Malloy

Published by **One Red Dog Press**

Portions of this book originally appeared in the *Bozeman Daily Chronicle* and *Montana Parent*. "Boys Will Be Boys" first appeared in *Family Circle*. Reprinted with permission.

Book design by Denise Malloy
Cover design by Denise Malloy
Author photo by Thomas Lee Photography
Make-up by Deirdre Quinn, Indulgence

Library of Congress Control Number: 2012901911

ISBN-13: 978-0615577319
ISBN-10: 0615577318

Printed in the United States of America

To
The Husband, Older Boy and Younger Boy

This book is dedicated to all the Real Mothers who do it everyday
with grace, style and quite often, spit-up on their shoulders.

FOREWARD

When you're a parent, the minutia piles up. This is the stuff that is of absolutely no interest to anyone except you and – if you're lucky – your spouse, but it's stuff that has to get done just the same.

Who is picking up which kid from what practice? How old is the milk in the refrigerator? The car insurance is going up how much? When is the last time someone let the dog out to pee?

All valid questions, to be sure. And, quite honestly, I don't recall anyone ever promising that raising a family would be for the meek. (I was, however, told that having two kids would be just as easy as one. Liars!)

Still, the days can meld into one another, your kids grow, and it's easy to lose sight of those wonderful moments that make it all worthwhile.

That's why I like the columns written by Denise Malloy.

Several years ago now, Denise started submitting a monthly column for *"Balance,"* a magazine focused on women's issues and published by the *Bozeman Daily Chronicle,* the newspaper for which I am currently the managing editor.

Denise wasn't writing about the national debt, or politics or taxes, which was just fine by me. Instead, her columns were about everyday life of being a mother and a wife here in our fair city of Bozeman, Montana. Her writing was typically relatable, often heartwarming and almost always funny as hell.

She was capturing those singular moments that make families what they are: loving and exasperating, hilarious and frustrating, but most of all, wonderful parts of each of us.

I thought her column deserved a wider audience, and once Denise came around to the appropriate conclusion that her editor is always right, she began writing more frequently for the daily newspaper itself. We've been lucky to have her.

There is a running joke in most newsrooms that inside every reporter is a book, and that's exactly where it should stay. Reading over Denise's columns, though, it's a fine body of work that holds up well to time, and I'm pleased that she has taken upon this project, *A Real Mother*.

The double meaning will not be lost on anyone who has enjoyed her columns.

— Nick Ehli, Managing Editor, *Bozeman Daily Chronicle*

Contents

Mom, Interrupted

"Hey Mom, where are my hockey skates?" "Hey Mom, have you seen my homework folder?" "Hey Mom, can I go to Jackson's house on Saturday?"

I have figured out why old people lose their hearing: it's because they want to. After raising children, they have used up their allotment of hearing for this lifetime. And they don't want to listen to anyone anymore about anything.

"Hey Mom, where's the glue?" "Hey Mom, do I have to practice piano?" "Hey, Mom, can you see somebody's soul?"

I have not had a complete thought in eleven years. Come to think of it, it's probably been twelve. It started when I was pregnant: clearly it must have been the hormones at work. Somehow during pregnancy, your brain starts to short circuit in preparation for the coming events of the child raising years, including sleep deprivation and your child's vocabulary development. Much like nature prepares your body for labor and delivery; hormones now help your brain develop Pause Waves, which cause all coherent thoughts to immediately vaporize upon formation.

It's probably a good thing.

"Hey Mom, what is a prism?" "Hey Mom, where's the milk?" "Hey Mom, did you get to ride the bus to school?"

It all begins shortly after birth as we coo over our adorable little bundles. Operating under the delusion that our child is a superior genius, we mentally transform a belch into our child's first complete sentence at about 8 weeks. Before long, when the authoritative parenting books tell us they should be using ten words, we're certain our child is beyond brilliant and is actually using 50 or 60 words. The reality is before long they really do know 300 words and they use them all - before you've had your first cup of coffee.

"Hey Mom, where do babies come from? Hey Mom, how long 'til Christmas? "Hey Mom, what's a square root?"

When they are babies, the interruptions are natural – the cry for *I need food, I need a clean diaper, I need to be held.* When they are toddlers, it is most often a matter of playing goalie as parent: catching them by the seat of the pants before they fall down the basement steps, grabbing their arm before they reach to pet the snarling dog, keeping them from walking into the street. But once they start talking the real interruptions flow freely and you may as well put away the books, magazines and newspapers as well as any hope of a coherent thought. You've just entered the Stream of Consciousness Zone of Parenting where every thought that enters your child's mind is verbalized the moment it hits the first brain cell. While your child's inner monologue will eventually develop, don't count on it anytime soon.

"Hey Mom, the dog just threw up on the carpet." "Hey Mom, can I have five dollars?" "Hey Mom, how long 'til I can learn how to drive?"

Most of the time, you think you can outsmart this immutable law of nature. But as you learn, one way or another, it is simply not possible. Once you've read the same paragraph seventeen times, you know it's over. If you are lucky, you might manage to read a caption in *People Magazine* in its entirety when they're in third grade. But for the most part, don't bother. You can read after they go to college.

"Hey Mom, have you seen my saxophone?" "Hey Mom, where's Ecuador?" "Hey Mom, how come the milk smells funny?"

Pretty soon, the lobes of your brain actually begin to shut down from lack of use. The lobes that remain functional now operate more like a strobe light. Your auditory nerve begins to shrivel and go limp like a long forgotten piece of celery. You fear that your ears might actually bleed if they tell you about that scene from *Star Wars* again.

"Hey Mom, did they have electricity when you were in school?" "Hey Mom, can I have some candy?" "Hey Mom, can we get a pet llama?"

But there will come a day and time when you can no longer stand the interruptions, whether it's from PMS, a bad day at work, or simply exasperation. The resonating sounds of your child's constant chatter threaten to reduce your ear canal's hammer, anvil and stirrup into a tiny pile of dust. Years of verbal tap dancing on the acoustic nerve will at some point shrink your patience to zero and you will snap. And just when you think that you can't take it anymore, that's when. . .

"Hey Mom. . ."

"WHAT??!!"

"I love you."

Livin' In The Hood

It's almost time for that special day to honor women who are livin' in the 'hood. Motherhood, that is. And for those of you who plan to pay tribute to a special mother you should know this: if you haven't been shopping yet, all the good Mother's Day cards are gone. But if the founder of this holiday, Anna Jarvis, had her way, we'd all be sitting down with a quill, ink and parchment to pen our ode to mother because a pre-printed ditty means you're just too lazy to show the love.

Lighten up Annie, it's the thought that counts.

I found it odd that the first official Mother's Day was celebrated in 1914. This is true despite the fact that women have been having babies since, well, the beginning of time. It took *that* long for someone to say "I really should do something to acknowledge the woman who carried me around for nine months, endured twenty-seven hours of labor, changed my stinky diapers, chauffeured me to soccer practice and raffled off a kidney to pay for my dream wedding. What can I possibly do to express my profound love to the woman who has given everything to me? I know, I'll give her a three dollar card from Hallmark."

Yeah, that sounds about right.

If you look at what a mom is really worth, you might reconsider that meager token of love. According to salary.com, a stay-at-home mom would receive $122,732 a year for all the duties she performs, which include being the Domestic CEO, housekeeper, chef, van driver, and psychologist. I don't know about you, but in fourteen years I've never seen a dime. Clearly we're not in it for the money. Because I've got a collection of handprints with glitter, macaroni glued in the shape of hearts and crayon declarations of love that are worth more to me than any paycheck. And that's just fine because glued and glittered love tokens are priceless.

Until I became a mom, I had no idea what my mother went through. The waiting started when she was pregnant and I was three weeks late. The waiting, as I've learned, never stops except you add worrying to the equation. She waited and worried when I got the Hong Kong Flu in 1968. She waited (and waited) while I took piano lessons and went to softball practice. Once I started driving, she waited up (and worried) when I was out too late at a Fleetwood Mac concert. She waited (and waited, but did not worry) when I had to try on every Gunne Sax dress in the store. Twice. She did not sell her spleen to finance my nuptials. But I'm pretty sure if I'd wanted a Cinderella-style gown, a horse drawn carriage and a pair of size nine glass slippers, she would have. Because that's just what mothers do.

Mom, I get it now.

So to all women in the sorority of motherhood, whether you had natural childbirth, an epidural, a C-section or boarded a long-haul flight to bring your baby home, you totally rock. You give it up unselfishly for those young 'uns every day (don't worry daddies, you do too, but your day's in June). Tomorrow is your day, moms.

Enjoy.

And I'm not worried if all the good cards are gone when I go shopping for my mom today. Because I'm pretty sure a Thank You card really says it all.

Identity Crisis

I used to have an individual personality. I had a career, hobbies, an identity all my own. But after I became pregnant, suddenly my individuality revolved around baby-to-be. Cheerful friends would ask, "How are WE feeling today?" Baby, apparently was just fine. I, on the other hand, had my head in the toilet from morning sickness that lasted 24/7 for the first trimester.

Once I started to show, which sadly was at about eight weeks, my identity revolved around my now extremely large belly, which would enter the room before I did. Other than the belly, it was as if I no longer existed. Complete strangers would walk up to me as if pulled by some huge magnet and place their hands on my tummy. Some would rub for a moment, as if waiting for secret communication from Baby. Others would touch my stomach briefly, close their eyes then announce, "Boy!" as if they'd just received divine gender guidance. I wanted to scream at them, "Hello? I'm attached over here. Hands off!" But it wouldn't have mattered anyway. At that moment, I had ceased to exist. I was Baby's Mom.

Then Baby arrived and that's when the fun really began. No one even noticed me anymore, which was perfect because sleep deprivation made me look like hell. People would coo over my adorable seven-pound wonder. But no more me. Denise as I had known her for 34 years had vaporized upon giving birth. As Baby's Mom, I was nothing more than a dispenser of milk, holder of baby and changer of diapers.

Once my babies entered school, I learned of my new identity on the motherhood highway: Schoolhouse Mom. My new nametag no longer read Denise. I was Older Boy and Younger Boy's Mom. Other parents you'd meet were associated with the accompanying kid. You might go through the elementary school years and not know any other parent by their real name. As Older Boy and Younger Boy's Mom, I quickly learned my new duties as Schoolhouse Mom: finder of all lost things, holder of backpacks, coats and lunchboxes.

Since Older Boy entered Middle School, no one needs to tell me the new identity I'm required to assume: Invisible Mom. I remember being mortified that someone would associate me with my parents, which was particularly stupid given that they had to drive me and my friends everywhere. But for me it got even worse. One morning, my mother was called to be the substitute teacher for my 6th grade class. Horrified, I begged her not to take the job that day. When I couldn't talk her out of showing up, I told her the only logical thing my 6th grade brain could think of. "Act like you don't know me," I hissed as we walked into the classroom.

Not only was I once a middle schooler (they called it junior high back then), but I actually taught this demographic long, long ago.

My 7th grade students would confide in me that they were quite certain that their parents were the dumbest, meanest and most embarrassing people on the planet. "They are SO MEAN, they never let me do ANYTHING," was the dramatic battle cry of my classroom full of 13-year-old walking hormones.

At least I felt a little more prepared for my new starring role as Invisible Mom. I know the rules – speak when spoken to, don't make eye contact. Don't talk, just drive. So when my son asked me to pick up a couple of his friends to go to the movies, I wasn't surprised when he launched into the dos and don'ts of the Unseen Parent. "Mom, don't say anything, okay?" Older Boy implored with a tone of alarm, knowing – quite correctly – that I could do or say something to completely embarrass him. "And whatever you do Mom, DON'T SING while they're in the car!" he admonished me.

And so too it had come to pass: I had become Invisible.

By the time they're in college, hopefully I'll shed my invisibility cloak. And I'm fairly certain they'll be looking for me when it's time to move on to my next identity in the life of a parent: College Tuition Paying Mom. Because that's one check they don't want signed in invisible ink.

Some Assembly Required

It's not the weather outside that's frightful. It's the language inside that has blossomed into something scary. The snow coming down does not compare to the profanity that now showers the family room in torrents. I'm afraid my children will wake up, hear this language swirling around the visions of sugarplums and wonder if Santa has sent one of the more surly elves to deliver the Christmas loot in our neighborhood.

It's that time of year again, 11 p.m. Christmas Eve, children tucked in their toasty beds dreaming of the morning's bounty to come. The Husband and I are repeating the scenario of years past, sitting crossed legged on the family room floor, surrounded by thousands of screws, washers, tiny plastic parts, and a few assorted tools that we have no idea how to use. The Husband is the original unhandyman and if I had my way, he wouldn't be allowed to operate more than a corkscrew. But putting the toys together is one of parenting's charming little chores. Just like changing diapers, like it or not, it must be done. The boxes scattered at my feet bear the three most feared words of the Christmas season: Some Assembly Required.

It amazes me that manufacturers can provide instructions in at least 27 languages, a few of which I believe are no longer in existence. Unfortunately, all of them are about as intelligible as anything written by the IRS. After wading through the indecipherable English directions, I become frantic, flipping through looking for something I can remotely recognize. I've tried to pair my rusty high school French with The Husband's college Spanish in an attempt to come up with something useful. But it usually turns into a guessing game based on the picture version of the directions for those among us who are assembly impaired. I've even tried to use the sketches that resemble something from the Lascaux Cave Paintings to assemble my child's Rockin' Drum Set. But from the picture, it looked like I needed a couple large, Paleolithic elk to hold the cymbals in place. Maybe a reindeer or two would do.

As in the past, we operate under the delusion that perhaps another glass of wine will help decipher the instructions. While the confidence and creativity in the assembly process do rise with consumption, I am sorry to report that there is an inverse correlation with precision, accuracy and most likely, personal safety.

Of course, why we wait until the midnight hour on Christmas Eve is beyond me. Maybe it's in hope that Santa will pop out from the chimney, observe the wretched scene and, in the true spirit of Christmas, offer to lend a hand to the less fortunate. Each year we vow at Thanksgiving that we'll get started early in the dreaded assembly of our gifts to the children. And once again, as in year's past, there we sit: sleepy, half-sloshed, sputtering profanities and fumbling with a few less pieces than the directions appear to require.

I'm always worried about our children actually using any presents that we've so pathetically tried to put together. It's disturbing to discover 5 or 6 large, important looking, leftover parts that didn't make it into the assembly process. I can only imagine Older Boy riding his new bike down the street and watching as the tires, seat, handlebars and finally my son, fall off onto the road. Or the cymbal launching off the Rockin' Drum Set like a Frisbee. We're just lucky we haven't had to go to the emergency room yet. By now The Boys should know to do a safety inspection of any presents from mom and dad. I'm surprised OSHA hasn't issued a memo to the Malloy household requiring the application of warning labels reading: DANGER: Toy Assembled By Mom And Dad: Use At Your Own Risk.

If I really planned ahead, I'd just ask Santa to send reinforcements. I'm not proud, I'll stand in line with the kids. I'll sit on his lap if I must.

I'm that desperate.

It is quite clear that we have ADD (Assembly Deficiency Disorder) and are in dire need of back-up. Surely the Big Man would show us a little compassion. It seems that a few of the boys from the elves' assembly department might want to earn a little overtime at our house.

Trust me, I'd pay a premium.

But after hearing our little outbursts over the years, I'm sure Santa will do little more than a drive-by to toss the kids' goodies on the curb. He might even pause long enough to throw a couple lumps of coal, Nolan Ryan-style, at our heads. Because after our Christmas Eve antics, we're going to be on the naughty list for a long, long time.

'Twas the Night Before Christmas

'Twas the night before Christmas
And all through the house
The only creatures stirring
Were me and my spouse

The kiddies were in bed
In a sleep that was deep
But The Husband and I had
Miles to go before sleep

It was Christmas Eve
And all across the land
Bleary-eyed parents
Could sure use a hand

Fumbling with tools
Long into the night
We hadn't a clue
If we were doing it right

When what to my wondering eyes
Did appear
But our favorite Chubby Guy
And his tiny reindeer

"Ho Ho Ho," he chuckled
With glee
"I'm glad that it's you
Putting those together, not me."

"Hey Santa," I said
"Please hurry come quick
Use whatever you can
A screwdriver or stick."

"Don't sweat it," he said
"You know I'm Da Man."
I said, "I don't care
Just do what you can."

"Listen, you clowns
It's worse than I feared
I've watched your blundering
Efforts each year."

"I've got you covered
St. Nick's got your back
I had such high hopes
But you two are toy-hacks."

"Just sit on the couch
It'll work out just fine
We'd all be much safer
If you'd both have some wine."

So Santa worked hard
Like a busy old elf
I couldn't believe
He did it all by himself

When the last screw was tightened
In an elegant display
He said, "Next year I'll come early
How's Thanksgiving Day?"

"Santa," I said, "Tell me
Sir, what can we do?"
'Leave the assembly to me," he cried,
"I repeat, never you!"

Then he boarded his sleigh
And hollered out of the blue
"Now I hate to relay
Your biggest snafu."

"You overlooked essentials
Now you're in a real fix
You forgot all the batteries
And Target closed at six."

Half The Fun Is Getting There

It's that time of year again – summer vacation. And if you're about to load up the family truckster and head down the road for some vacation fun, I have a word of advice.

Don't.

Because time after time, I am bamboozled into agreeing that we should drive to our destination. "We'll have a great time," The Husband lies, channeling Clark Griswald.

And I believe him.

Apparently I'm an idiot. Because it always turns into a disaster.

Like the road trip when Older Boy was seven. As we snaked up a curvy mountain pass Older Boy announced, "I have to throw up." I chalked it up to boredom, especially knowing his penchant for more drama than trauma. "Use this," I said, handing him a Starbucks paper bag with twine handles. "Look, you can hang it on your ears," I told him giving a smug wink to The Husband. Older Boy carefully placed the handles behind each ear.

Then he threw up.

When I looked back, Older Boy was sitting calmly. Knowing the closest place to safely pull over was the Scenic Mountain Lookout three miles away, I said, "We're pulling ov- . . ."

Before I could finish, Older Boy interrupted. "Mom, the bag broke," he said matter-of-factly with the now bottomless bag still hanging from his ears.

Didn't see that coming.

Barf and I do not have a happy history. Ever since Lisa Lapinski threw up on my brown and white saddle shoes in first grade, one whiff and I start sympathy gagging. I am useless when someone in my vicinity hurls, unless you count dry heaves as somehow helpful.

The Husband cleaned up Older Boy and the mess while I offered support in the form of a chorus of retching. I drove since I'd have an unobstructed view with my head hanging out the window.

The barf-covered clothes took on a new DNA permeating life force as they baked in the back window. It was at that moment, when I thought the stench inside the car couldn't get any worse, that I rounded a curve and ran right over a bloated critter carcass releasing a new and more potent noxious gas into the vehicle. The good news was I forgot about the vomit smell. The bad news is I had to torch my clothes before the hotel would let me check in.

I should have gone home. But somehow, even on the most horrible road trips, I remain ridiculously optimistic.

So the next morning, we headed for the beach. Believing the

worst of this road trip was behind us, we pulled into the hotel on a gorgeous day. I sensed that The Husband wanted to share a male bonding moment with The Boys so I went for supplies.

I took my time, knowing we couldn't check in for hours. But as I walked out of the Mariner's Mart, the sky had turned into an ominous gray quilt. As I drove, the light rain turned into a downpour. When I pulled into the parking lot, there they were, seeking shelter under the Dog Relief Area sign. Looking more closely, I could see a bottom lip quivering slightly.

And that was just The Husband.

Arms crossed, shirts and shorts salt stained from the ocean, they all stared straight ahead, ignoring one other. "I wanna go home," Younger Boy whined. "Me too," Older Boy chimed in. "I'll drive," The Husband said.

So the next time The Husband offers to drive on vacation, just like always, I'll let him. As long as it's to the airport.

The World According to Granny

When I got married, my mother's biological clock started ticking. Her Grandmother Biological Clock, that is. Every year, she'd point out the obvious - we were still childless. "All my friends ARE grandparents," she would tell me. "Get pregnant already."

So eight years later when my mother learned she was going to become a grandmother, she wistfully sighed, "My life is complete." As my belly grew, she impatiently waited for the arrival of her Meaning of Life. And waited. And waited. Because in keeping with family tradition, Older Boy was late.

Over two weeks late.

My mother grew ansty. As she crossed the days off past my Christmas Day due date, she became downright belligerent. "Have that baby already," she practically yelled into the phone. "I'm tired of waiting!"

She wasn't the only one.

But the moment she folded back the blanket in which he was

wrapped like a baked potato, counted ten fingers and toes, my mother declared him Perfect. And no other child on the face of the planet would ever be as Perfect, at least until Younger Boy came along.

So what's the grandmother of the Two Most Perfect Children on the Planet to do? Exactly what grandmothers down through the ages have done: tell EVERYONE about them.

Mom would call to tell me about lunch with the ladies and her obvious efforts at Grandma-One-Up-Manship. I can just see them sitting around the lunch table like it's a game of Texas Hold 'Em, each one keeping the best story in the hole.

Because the stakes can get high.

But to me, my mother's fantastical tales of her grandsons as viewed through her Granny Goggles sounded more like my dad's best fishing stories.

So it's no surprise that my mother plays her hand like a Vegas pro. I just never expected it to happen so soon. "I told them how he's already reading!" she gushed. "Do you have *War and Peace*? I'm sending it."

"Mom, he's seven months old," I explained logically. "He drools on the book and chews the pages. He's NOT reading."

"That's because it's not *War and Peace*," she said smugly. "It's in the mail. Give it to him or you're out of the will."

When they started school, it only got worse. I mailed her a picture Younger Boy drew in kindergarten that was a mishmash of random yellow and blue scribbles. The teacher had written "Night" on it.

My mother called as soon as she came in from the mailbox. "It's brilliant. A masterpiece," she said. "He's a little Vincent, I tell you. I know these things."

"Mom, it's random yellow and blue Crayola marks," I said. "It's a cute kindergarten drawing, but he's no Van Gogh."

"I'm calling MOMA. They'll want to display this next to the original," she said just before hanging up on me.

I suspect it's only going to get worse. I'm certain at lunch one day when Girlfriend Granny opens with "My grandson got the results from his SAT test. He scored in the top 5%." Granny to the left will chuckle softly, raise an eyebrow and call her bet with, "Mine got a PERFECT score." And my poker-faced mother, without even looking up from buttering her roll, will raise the pot by nonchalantly throwing in, "Mine WROTE the SAT."

Although my mother never taught me the rules of poker, I'll still be able to play the Grandma Game one day. Because I learned from my dad that there's nothing quite like a good fish tale.

Now You're Talkin' Teen

We had just pulled up in front of Younger Boy's school. "Mom!" he announced with enthusiasm uncharacteristic for that time of morning, "That kid's in my social studies class. He's SO ill!"

Hearing about what I imagined was a hacking, snot-nosed and quite possibly feverish kid sitting next to mine was not a great way to start my day. "What do you mean he's *ill*?" I asked without waiting for a reply. "Why is a sick kid coming to school? I mean seriously, what are his parents thinking anyway? If he's ill, he should be at the doctor's office, not sneezing on his classmates! And shouldn't the school just send him right back home before he makes everyone else sick?"

After my rant subsided, a slightly uncomfortable silence fell over the car. "Mom, you just don't get it," he said.

Pause for Younger Boy's dramatic eye roll just before he slammed the door.

Talk about lost in translation.

Of course, I once spoke the teen vernacular. But that was back when I was one. At that time, I was standing next to our piece of television furniture the size of a Buick on harvest gold shag carpet in the middle of our Early American themed living room. I remember telling my mom that I was psyched because I had enough bread for some new threads. For me, this turn of events while making a whopping $2.10 an hour was Far Out. But my mother didn't Catch My Drift. And you should've seen the baffled look on my Dad's face when I asked him "Can you dig it?" without having a shovel in my hand. This was when I would Book Outta There, Keep On Truckin' till I arrived and Catch Ya On The Flip after I left. And there was a time when I thought my pet rock was pretty awesome.

For awhile in the 80s, I remained fluent in teen. I taught those walking hormones, commonly known as seventh graders, who roamed the gnarly hallways of Iroquois Middle School. I was the cool teacher because I would let my kids bring their boom boxes, which were too enormous to fit in a locker, so they could practice their break dancing on the tattered remains of a refrigerator box. It was totally righteous, dude.

Word.

So I thought it would be wise to get myself up to speed on the baffling slanguage of today's teen so I could be a totally fly, modern mom.

What a noob.

But that's when I found *Good Housekeeping's* online, Test Your Teen Slang Quiz. Needless to say, I was stoked when I understood that Let's Bounce didn't mean a basketball. And while I did grasp the notion of Chillin', I didn't have the slightest clue about what made one an Emo.

Pwned again.

I was more than surprised when my score indicated that I was down with my teen's lingo. Because of my supposed mastery of youthful linguistics, the *Good Housekeeping* quiz bestowed upon me the title of Coolest Mom, Ever.

As if.

I'm sure my kids would agree that I'll never be in the running for that sash and tiara that comes with winning the title of Coolest Mom. I'll never be fly. I'll always be a little phat thanks to my genetics. The most bling I'm comfortable with is my resurfaced hip.

And that's just groovy, baby.

Joy in Mudville

Spring is in the air, the days are longer and the grass is green. And that means it's time for the annual rite of passage for parents known as t-ball.

This is the time for the 4 to 8 year-old set to learn how to throw, hit and catch. So I felt duty-bound to sign up Older Boy when he was five.

I think participation is actually required by federal law.

After sitting on the sidelines that season, I decided it would be even more fun if we made it a family endeavor since Younger Boy was now old enough to play. I thought being a t-ball coach would be a cinch, so I signed The Husband up.

Signing your spouse up for a volunteer commitment with a group of individuals who do not yet have all their permanent teeth is never a good idea. But I persisted.

"Wouldn't it be more fun than just sitting there?" I argued. "And don't worry about doing it all by yourself, I'll help you.

Besides, it's just t-ball, how hard can it be?"

Does there ever come a point in your life when you stop asking this incredibly stupid question?

At the coaches' meeting, The Husband picked up a duffel bag of bats, balls, bases, a hitting tee and the roster. I had the most important task - picking out the t-shirt color for our team.

At the first practice, I bribed the five and six-year-olds with juice boxes and sat them in a shady spot under a tree where The Husband was going to introduce the fundamentals of the game to his eager audience. My job was to meet with the parents to discuss their vital role during season: Snack Duty.

As The Husband began his introductory speech, he sounded suspiciously like Ebby Calvin LaLoosh in *Bull Durham*. "T-ball is a simple game," he said enthusiastically. "We hit the ball. We catch the ball. We throw the ball." The kids looked at The Husband with a level of concentration last seen by Sparky Anderson during Game 6 of the 1975 World Series in Fenway Park. I watched in amazement. These kids were serious.

This was going to be hardball.

A tiny girl with enormous blue eyes raised her hand. "I have a puppy," she announced and ran off towards the swing set. Two others followed.

Oh well.

Several practices later it was Game Day. I was to sit with the kids and maintain order, which amounted to me working them into a general frenzy with knock-knock jokes. My other job was to help them remember THE MOST IMPORTANT T-BALL RULE EVER:

DON'T THROW THE BAT.

Puppy Girl hit the ball on the first try. She didn't slow down as she raced past first base and headed straight for the swing set. The next batter smacked the ball and ran to third. During our turn in the outfield, it didn't get much better. The left fielder sat down and picked dandelions. The second baseman picked his nose. The centerfielder was doing the Hokey Pokey and made a fabulous play just before she put her whole self in. The third baseman broke into a theatrical version of *I Just Can't Wait To Be King*. His mom hid behind a cooler of melting popsicles.

Puppy Girl was up again. She hit the ball, ran to first and broke into a victory dance standing right on top of the base.

And at that moment, my friends, there was finally Joy in Mudville.

Axe the Axe

Santa, dear Santa
It's that time of year
But you showing up
Is now my biggest fear

I'm not being critical
Of the stuff that you bring
In fact, I'll tell you
It's only one thing

Santa, you know
I don't mean to be mocking
But last time you left
This stuff in the stocking

So Santa, my friend
I've just one thing to say
Please don't leave Axe
At my house Christmas Day

Santa, it's hard
For the mother of boys
It was so much easier
When you just left them toys

But now as young men
They want to smell good
I only wish
That they understood

That Axe is plain nasty
It smells awfully rank
Between you and me
I'd rather they stank

Axe is disgusting
I don't mean to nag
Walk into a cloud of it
And you'll surely gag

Santa, my dear
I don't mean to be rude
But after they spray it
I can't taste my food

But Santa, it's true
And you and I know
There's a much better way
To get rid of B.O.

The answer's not Axe
So please grant my wish
Cause I think they'd smell better
If they rolled in dead fish

It's really quite simple
Santa, don't be a dope
If you want them to smell good
Just bring towels and some soap.

Shifting into Panic Mode

The time has finally come. It's the day I've dreaded from the moment that First Response announced *You're Pregnant* with Older Boy. I'm starting to think those words pale in comparison to the two words that are suddenly about to rock my world with Older Boy. The two words that have struck fear in my heart for the last fifteen years: Driver's Ed.

In a few short weeks, Older Boy will take his place behind the wheel. My insurance agent can't stop smiling.

These days, the process is straightforward. Leave it to the professionals. Sign up for Driver's Ed and let a patient instructor sit beside your child the first time they buckle his or her seat belt in the driver's seat.

My parents weren't quite so lucky.

In a school without Driver's Ed, the only thing I could do as I closed in on my Sweet Sixteen was pore over the driver's manual. I memorized road signs. I could recite traffic laws. I knew stopping distances by heart. Nothing was going to come between my and my coveted Learner's Permit.

On my birthday, my Mom dropped me off at the DMV. I nervously circled the answers with my No. 2 pencil and fidgeted while the lady behind the desk graded my test. When she handed me back the paper with a smile, I thought I would be driving out of the parking lot. Instead she said, "We need to check your vision."

I thought I squinted my way to a respectable degree of distance vision. The Commonwealth of Kentucky didn't see it that way. "Honey, come back after you get glasses," the lady said through a haze of cigarette smoke.

So instead of me piloting our Ford Falcon off to a celebratory milkshake, my Mom drove me to the eye doctor who confirmed the DMV's diagnosis of extreme near-sightedness with astigmatism thrown in for good measure. A few weeks later, I left the doctor's office with Coke bottle thick glasses in a groovy Jan Brady-style.

I returned to the DMV, this time actually able to read the sign behind the desk, where the same lady handed me my Learner's Permit. When she stamped CORRRECTIVE LENSES across it in red ink, the ash nearly fell off her cigarette dangling from her lips. My Mom handed me the keys. "You can drive us home," she said.

It was the first and last time I drove with her in the car while I had my permit.

Apparently, my Mom thought that the piece of paper somehow conveyed the ability to operate a motor vehicle by osmosis. Because I didn't have a clue. On that short, yet white-knuckled ride, my now wild-eyed Mom clutched the door as she worked an imaginary brake on the passenger side as I careened down the road.   When my Dad got home from work, my Mom was lying on the couch with a washrag on her head, groaning.

"I see you got your permit," he said to me.   "Let's go to Kmart."

In that parking lot over the course of a few weeks, my Dad never lost his cool while patiently teaching me how to stop without giving us whiplash, make turns smoothly and drive a stick shift without killing it.   He told me to always signal, use my mirrors and to never, ever panic in the car.

So far, he's been right.

But I'll leave the upcoming driving instruction to the professionals and The Ever-Patient Husband.   Because despite my Dad's lessons, when it comes to Older Boy and driving, I know the only thing I'll be able to shift into is panic mode.

Becoming Mother

Upon exiting the shower, I was startled to find my mother in the bathroom. "Mom, when did you get into town?" I inquired of the middle-aged woman who was staring at me. As the steam cleared, her identity was revealed and I shrieked when I learned the truth. –

It was me.

Without warning, the unthinkable had happened: I had become my mother. When I told my mom, she laughed uncontrollably. Shortly afterwards, a present from her arrived: a sassy statue holding a sign that said "It's official. I've become my mother!"

Many of us think we can outrun that powerful pull of our genes. "It won't happen to me," I smugly thought. But as the years began to unfold, so did those little strands of DNA that tied me inextricably to my foremothers.

The first signs that those wisps of my genetic material were beginning to unravel in their trek towards self-expression began a few years ago. Without warning, I became enchanted with all things sparkly, much like a crow with an affinity for aluminum foil. Although my mother never met a sequin she didn't love, this clearly dates back to my grandmother who purchased her first BeDazzler in the 70s and wasn't afraid to use it. Everything in her house, including my grandfather, who looked ready to perform on the *Grand Old Opry*, was embellished with those colorful fake stones. Not only was her fashion inspired by gleaming adornments, but also her personal grooming. I recall being severely traumatized after one of her adventures with hair care products. When I was seven, she picked me up at school looking more like an escapee from the set of Goldfinger than my grandmother. In a fit of apparent whimsy, she'd spray painted her spiffy beehive hairdo gold.

Grandma Kate merged her love of gaudy with her love of shopping by wholeheartedly embracing the Home Shopping Network. But this had the unintended effect of underscoring her propensity for malapropisms, another genetic gem in my colorful maternal lineage. A devotee of QVC, grandma would call me to let me know a gift was forthcoming. She'd squeal with delight relaying my good fortune, "I got you a new set of *segregated* knives."

The Diamonique portion of QVC brought forth the opportunity to bedeck her only granddaughter in all manner of things sparkly with the convenience of four easy payments. "It's so beautiful," she said in a reverent tone, "you'd never guess it was a *stimulated* diamond."

My mother has proudly continued the linguistic family tradition. She recently relayed the details of her colon-*ostomy* and the pain in dad's *rotary cup*. She also recounted an episode of her favorite Food Network show. "I learned how to make candy," she explained. "Don't you ever watch *Emerald*?"

Much to my horror, I discovered that I, too, had started my mid-life trek down the malaprop highway. Feeling rather hip, I purchased a new CD. "Check it out, I got the new one from K. *D. Turnstile*," I told The Boys. Older Boy looked at me like he was fairly certain he was not my spawn and corrected me, enunciating very slowly, "Mom, it's K. T. Tunstall." He then rolled his eyes and left the room.

So when mom's most recent phone call gave me another gene alert, I wasn't surprised. "I just got home from my physical. The doctor said I have the blood pressure of a 30 year-old and the bones of a 20 year-old," Mom reported with understandable pride. "The doctor told me that so many women go downhill as they get older but *I just* keep getting better." Now it's pretty obvious that I've dipped my toes into that sparkly, linguistically challenged end of my maternal gene pool and that's just fine by me. Because if I get the package deal on this gene thing, then I'm one lucky woman.

Lil' Fashionistas

According to *Time Magazine*, the latest market for designer clothing is toddler to elementary school-aged kiddos. Of course, this seems entirely logical since that demographic has loads of disposable income. The article states that high-end designer jeans in sizes that end in Ts are being snapped up at 150 bucks a pop. It's clear that these fashion designers are taking the demands of status conscious parents straight to the bank.

I guess baby really does need new (designer) shoes.

Apparently our youngsters are turning into pint-sized fashionistas. Kids as young as the kindergarten set are now actively involved in choosing attire that articulates their fashion image to the world. I realize that kids do feel the need to express themselves when it comes to their clothing. But when my kids (granted they are boys) felt the need to communicate their fashion style, it was usually by some visually offensive combination of plaids and stripes or insisting on wearing their too small Superman jammies, rainboots and a holster to the grocery. If my four-year-old would have refused to get dressed unless he was wearing a $99 Little Marc Button-Down Cotton Surfer Dude Shirt and $150 Diesel Jeans, I would have correctly assumed he fell out of his toddler bed right on his head.

At what point did developing fashion sophistication by age 5 turn up on the parenting menu? When did a $225 Dolce & Gabbana Linen Safari dress become necessary for little missy to go to finger paint another kid at day care? Can you even fathom putting any baby, particularly a puker, in a $300 Little Marc cashmere sweater? Although he will look precious, considering that punkin' will grow out of those 2T Lit'l Ernie jeans in a few months, is it logical to spend $125 on them? Unless your darling is already a runway model, or worse, a future Little Miss Sunshine, is a $400 Alberta Ferretti "flirty" chiffon dress even appropriate?

Apparently some later-life parents have lost a little something more than their youthful figures in the pregnancy process: they've completely lost their common sense.

In the article, a member of a market research group said, ". . . the fact that you can't tell them what to wear is really driving the market." Hello? Check the birth certificate, you are the parent. Like it or not, this means you are in charge of that pesky little parenting thing. That means you get to call the shots (including those involving the purchase of clothing), make the decisions and use the word *No*. You, in short, ARE the boss of them. Unless your adorable toothless one manages to bring home the bacon, even though he may not yet be able to chew it, I'd say you pretty much have free reign in establishing your tot's fashion budget. You could also choose to use my dad's three favorite words when I would whine for something beyond the limits of our family's fiscal reality: Get a Job.

If we choose to succumb to the unreasonable demands of the snot-nosed set, what will they require next? Strappy Manolo Blanhnik gym shoes ($375) that say "I'm ready to play but still just a little sassy?" A Juicy Couture Little Diva Backpack ($425) to tote sweetpea's homework to school?

Gives a whole new meaning to Bratz.

The article concludes that both boomer and celebrity moms want the very best for their kids. Well, duh. Color me naïve, but I've always operated under the misguided impression that what's best for our kids meant giving them plenty of our time, attention and the knowledge that they are loved, not designer duds. Besides, if anyone in my house is wearing apparel that doesn't sport a Target label, you can bet it's going to be me.

Road Trip

Long ago and far away, in a land before Garmins, Magellans and Tom-Toms, there was only one way to assure getting from point A to point B on your vacation. There was no Mapquest to plan your route and estimated driving time. The most common travel partner was the virtually useless rectangular map from the Shell Gas Station, which once unfolded became an unwieldy beast with a life of its own. Of course, these maps would never again be neatly refolded into that compact little parallelogram: after several frustrating attempts the awkward creature would be wadded into a ball and stuffed under the passenger seat.

Apparently my family was incapable of ad-libbing it en route to our annual beach outing, even though we went to the same hotel at the same beach the same week every year via the same stretch of interstate roadway. According to my Dad, there was only one way to properly get to your destination: the AAA Trip Tik. Dad never ventured outside Jefferson County, Kentucky without the benefit of one of those spiral bound, multi-page navigational wonders.

Dad would call the friendly folks at AAA months before our departure date. He'd pick up our trip planner complete with each state's fold out maps in the event that you inadvertently strayed off-course from the green highlighted stretch of road. Everything was conveniently stuffed into a tiny garbage bag for the trip, which Dad would hang on the cigarette lighter with a flourish the morning of our departure signaling Houston, We Have Lift Off.

After picking up the Trip Tik, Dad would ceremoniously gather us around the kitchen table to go over our route much like I imagine Vasco de Gama assembling the armada for a quick nautical briefing before shoving off around the Cape of Good Hope. "Clear from Louisville to E-town, good," Dad would say carefully turning each page and running his finger down the highlighted stretch of I-65. "Ah-ha! Looky what we have here. There's construction in Nashville! I knew it!" Dad seemed to think that the Tennessee Department of Transportation had some personal vendetta against him and purposely scheduled road repair closures and detours during our annual trek. "If we didn't have this," he'd say fondly patting page 3, "we just might not make it." Now admittedly the re-routing and construction delays were annoying, but even at my tender age I seriously doubted that our trip would be DOA because of a Road Closed sign in the Music City.

We sat as Dad carefully reviewed each page with us. But I never figured out the purpose of this part of the ritual because my mother steadfastly refused to drive outside the city limits and I couldn't see over the dashboard. Apparently it was in case one of us was forced to pilot the Cutlass Supreme through the diabolical traffic maze of Opp, Alabama after an unscheduled pit stop. Every night until our departure, Dad would retire to his Barcalounger to study each page of the Trip Tik as if he was preparing for a NASA moon landing instead of driving the wife and kid to Panama City Beach.

When I was nine, I thought the Trip Tik was pretty cool, especially when I got to be the co-pilot during the non-critical portions of our trip between places like Cash Point, Tennessee and Blount Springs, Alabama. But by the time I was thirteen, I realized that I could have probably taken the helm if I knew how to work the clutch. "Dad, why do you need that dumb thing," I'd say in that oh-so obnoxious way mastered by thirteen-year-olds. "You practically get on I-65 in our driveway and you hang a left until you see the Gulf of Mexico. How hard can it be?" I paused for dramatic effect, "And besides, Dad, it's just so uncool!"

Suddenly Dad morphed into Kung Fu's Master Po. "Perhaps we will try it your way, grasshopper," he said in a calm voice of worldly experience. "You, wise young teenager, will guide us to the beach this year."

So in my I'm-thirteen-and-I-know-everything kind of way, I took Dad's challenge to become the family's Chief Navigational Officer. And I'm happy to report that with me at the helm we had our most memorable vacation ever: in downtown Nashville.

Count on It

It looked like any other afternoon as my 4th grade son started his math homework at the kitchen table. Even when he asked for help, all was still well as I walked over with confidence.

Until I saw the problem.

As I looked at the paper, my palms began to sweat and my heart began to race (cue *Psycho* shower scene music). This was no ordinary equation; this was my nemesis - the dreaded Algebra Word Problem. Exactly when did they start dropping A-bombs in the 4th grade? I first flunked, I mean took, algebra in high school.

For Indiana Jones, it was snakes. For me, my biggest fear is all things math. It's been that way since Mrs. DePew humiliated me in the 4th grade. What little math self esteem I had left was promptly squashed by my 5th grade teacher's sensible shoes. From that moment, that tiny lobe of my brain responsible for numerical operations shriveled like a forgotten grape in my refrigerator. And that portion of my brain has remained inert ever since. Any task I have to perform related to numbers as an adult requires a calculator, plenty of sharpened #2 pencils and a shot of bourbon. Then I call my accountant.

Apparently I'm not the only arithmophobe out there. In the world of phobias, death, public speaking and spiders are in the top ten with math. Half of Americans claim to have some fear of math, many of whom saw *A Beautiful Mind*. Half of Americans are good at math and I am thankful because I need all the help I can get. The other half of Americans fall into that proverbial gray area of all things numerical – they fear public speaking about math. (Now before your slide rule slips a digit, I know that doesn't add up – the correct formula to get the total number of math phobes in this country is the square root of a rhombus divided by 2x.)

I fear death by algebra.

Don't get me wrong, I like Xs and Ys just fine, in words or chromosomes, but never, ever as part of the world of numbers. Have you ever used an X or a Y in your checkbook?

I didn't think so.

So I rely on The Husband to ride in on the white horse to rescue me from the ambush of Xs and Ys. But this has created yet another, unique math problem that I didn't count on: Old School Math Daddy helping in a New Math World. Back when Math Daddy went to school, Sister Agnes taught math the old fashioned way: Don't Make Me Use the Ruler. Sister Agnes firmly believed that long division had been performed the same way since cave children carved their homework on stone tablets. So learn it, live it, love it. Or else.

So when Math Daddy tried to apply the Sister Agnes method of math instruction, Older Boy grew even more frustrated. "But Dad, you're doing it wrong!" he said. Math Daddy continued patiently, "There's only one way to do long division." This apparently was not reassuring. "I know and you're doing it wrong!" Older Boy cried. Finally, Math Daddy lost it. "Listen up, Archimedes, they've been doing math this way since Euclid first postulated a theorem," he said.

Math Daddy was starting to channel Sister Agnes.

Sensing that the rational voice of logic and reason might be helpful at this juncture, I intervened. "Let's take turns," I said trying to channel Mr. Rogers. "Why don't you show Dad how the teacher did it, then Dad can show you his way?" I'm happy to report that the homework was completed without further interference from Spirits of Math Past. But it only served to reinforce my fears. Why do you think they're called irrational numbers?

Preconceived Notions

We've really become a nation of control freaks as parents: we want it Our Way and We Want It Now. Somehow we've been led to believe that Have it Your Way applies not just to fast-food burgers, but to parenting. To me, nothing illustrates this point more clearly than the trend for an expectant generation of helicopter parents-in-training: Birth Plans.

I'm the first to admit that I'm a Sikorsky when it comes to my mom duties. So naturally, when the first eleven test sticks revealed double blue lines affirming that baby was on board, I vowed to be in the driver's seat of this little parental adventure. In short, I was going to be in charge.

Har de har har.

Nature was kind enough to let me *think* that my preconceived notions mattered long enough to write up that little labor and delivery manifesto. I smugly handed my Labor Day Treatise to my doctor and everyone at the hospital, including a pleasant guy manhandling a floor buffer in the lobby. My birth plan looked more like a ransom note and should have been constructed from words cut from discarded magazines. "No C-section. No Drugs. Peaceful, natural labor and delivery." Let's just say my delusional vision of the birth experience didn't quite coincide with what nature had in store.

So it should have been no surprise when baby's due date came and went without so much as a Braxton-Hicks contraction to commemorate the occasion. Two weeks later, it was clear that baby wasn't about to budge. He was fed, he was comfortable, and he wasn't going anywhere in the near future (much like I imagine him at 25 and still living in my basement.) By that time, I looked like I was ready to give birth to Gary Coleman.

The doctor informed me it was time to take action. "Looks like you need a little help," she advised. "No drugs," I whined. My eyes glazed over until I realized what she was really doing. "You're trying to SCARE me into labor, right?" I asked. "If you don't have that baby by Monday, we're going to induce," she told me in an I-Am-Not-Joking tone.

I decided I didn't need any help; this was a do-it-yourself project. Labor? Bring it on. So armed with a bottle of castor oil and a sack of spicy burritos, I put Project Labor into action. After downing that, I waddled around the block and waited for the onslaught of contractions. The only thing that delightful combo induced was a bad case of gas.

With the bun still in the oven now overcooking, I sheepishly reported to the hospital Monday afternoon. Not only did I require drugs, I required an emergency C-section. I was anything but peaceful as I shrieked at the anesthesiologist, "NATURAL CHILDBIRTH ONLY!" He wisely shrugged and slapped the mask over my mouth before I could get any louder. At that moment the only thing my birth plan was good for was hamster cage liner.

So when baby number two was riding shotgun, I revamped my original ill-conceived plans. "Drugs?" my doctor inquired. "Yes, please," I replied. "Can we start 'em now?" She then said in a reassuring tone, "You don't have to plan on a C-section this time." I whipped out my pocket calendar. "Yes. I. Do." I said. "Pencil me in. How about a Wednesday?" And 38 weeks later, I arrived at the hospital at 6 a.m. on that Wednesday morning. At 8:24 a.m., I was holding wrinkled, screaming baby number 2, right on schedule.

Now THAT was a plan.

So Parents-to-Be, plan if you dare. But don't be too upset when things veer off course while sailing the high seas of pregnancy. Because once the sperm and egg start their little square dance of love, Mother Nature calls all the shots. And that's exactly how She planned it.

Frazzled Mom – Then and Now

As I loaded my groceries in the car, I noticed the woman parked next to me was doing the exact same thing. But I finished first. I had the distinct advantage because she was Frazzled Mom – doing it while trying to keep two high-octane, toddler-age boys within arm's reach. Her lightening fast footwork was like watching Pele work the ball just before slamming it into the back of the net with a bicycle kick.

I watched as Frazzled Mom placed a bag in the trunk then sprinted off to grab the giggling 4-year-old who had decided to climb up the light post. By the time she corralled him, the younger boy had dashed off to go for a heart-stopping ride on a nearby basket. When I heard the click of the second car seat, I was fairly certain I would see the now triumphant Frazzled Mom sliding on her knees across the parking lot much like Brandi Chastain's famous 1999 Women's' World Cup sports bra revealing moment. But unlike super-fit Brandi with six-pack abs, all real mothers know why kneeling Frazzled Mom didn't rip her shirt off in her moment of victory.

Stretch marks.

I had to chuckle as I stood there surveying this scene of motherhood. Because as I watched, I was magically transported back to the year 2000 – when The Boys were 2 and 4. And I was Frazzled Mom playing goalie for two rowdy toddlers in my own personal World Cup of Parenting. And most of the time I was losing.

I shudder to think what the well-groomed women of Rochester, New York thought when I'd roll into the parking lot and unload my boisterous brood. Younger Boy always clamored loudly to be the first one out. But Mom Logic told me to get Older Boy out first, because being the oldest he was more likely to listen and follow directions.

Dare to dream.

I'd release Older Boy, then immediately break into a dead run as he sprinted across the parking lot laughing hysterically. When I'd finally retrieved him, I'd return to spring a now even louder Younger Boy from his car seat prison. The scene would immediately replay with me chasing Younger Boy, this time while toting 37-pound Older Boy under one arm. By the time I rounded them both up, I'd completely forgotten why we were even there.

I tried to solve my parking lot dilemma by reasoning with The Boys. I bribed them. I threatened them.

And when all that failed, in a moment of complete and total parental exasperation, I reached an epiphany in my parking lot quandary.

I screamed, "PUT YOUR HANDS ON THE CAR! NOW!"

To my surprise, and unlike any episode of *COPS* I've ever seen, they both froze – with their hands on the car.

At that moment, everyone in Wegman's parking lot swiveled their heads to look for the woman shrieking in a Southern accent. When they saw my 1984 Grand Marquis with blown front shocks, I'm sure they were expecting to see me wearing an *I'm a Redneck Woman* tank top, with a dangling bra strap, while chasing The Boys who were clad in Lil' NASCAR Driver T-shirts, fully loaded diapers while sucking on baby bottles filled with Mountain Dew.

Even though my World Cup of Parenting had morphed into something resembling a shocking *COPS* moment, the moms who just endured that spectacle knew they'd be safe from viewing at least one thing – my stretch marks.

Boys Will Be Boys

"The kids seem a little wired today," The Husband says when I call to check on them. I tell him, "Must be spring fever, I'll be home in a bit," chuckling as I hang up the phone. Now he's getting a taste of my days.

As I walk in the door, I hear them in the basement. The house is utterly spotless upstairs. He must be more organized than I am, I think to myself. I hear The Boys giggling as I head down the steps to say hello, completely unprepared for what I am about to see.

My two- and four-year-old sons, one in a diaper, the other in his underwear, are running around shooting a basketball at two plastic, kid-sized hoops. In between each shot, they jump up and down on a crib mattress, which for some indiscernible reason is right in the middle of the makeshift court. The Boys are cackling like this is the most fun they've had in weeks. I scan the room for signs of candy or empty soda cans as the source of their high-octane behavior.

None.

But I do see half-empty bowls of pretzels and popcorn, and a couple of empty sippy cups littering the floor. Then I catch sight of The Husband, lying on the couch watching the NCAA basketball semifinals, completely oblivious to the spectacle taking place before my eyes. I momentarily wonder if perhaps The Boys have tied him up. Finally, he shifts his gaze from the players on the screen to me. I fight the urge to yell, "What the hell is going on here?" As the shock subsides, I realize that what is going on is the living, breathing, giggling difference between how mothers and fathers parent.

I never really notice it when the four of us are together. But the difference becomes apparent when I'm gone for the day. When I return home I feel as if I have entered the kids' version of *Animal House*, a wild day at the fraternity with the boys, just the boys.

I'm a stay-at-home mom and The Boys and I have our little routine. Predictable, but not altogether boring. We play, we cook, we color, we talk. I think we have a pretty good time. But when I am gone, suddenly our house turns into an amusement park complete with Goofy, The Husband, as tour director.

As I stand in my basement surveying the wreckage, Older Boy says, "Mom, let me show you what Dad taught us today. Hey, Dad, come on, let's show Mom." The Boys, still without clothes on, grin at one another, and I wonder if they execute a secret handshake when they are out of my line of sight. The two of them drag the crib mattress to the top of the stairs.

I stare in disbelief as my two-year-old cascades down the

steps on the mattress, laughing hysterically. The look I give The Husband clearly says, "What are you doing?" The Husband looks back at me sheepishly and answers as if he has read my mind: "we were just having fun." His tone implies that perhaps at that moment I don't know how to do so. I am taken aback slightly by the remark. Then I break into laughter right along with them, partly at the spectacle of a theme park ride created right in my home, but also at the distinct difference in parenting styles that I see before me. Boys will be boys, and some boys will never quite grow up when given the chance to play.

Maybe that's a good thing.

I wonder what this difference stems from and why it only surfaces when I leave the house. Is there some primal testosterone thing at work here? A male-bonding experience that cannot occur when ovaries are present?

Being the only female in my house, save for two spayed dogs, I cannot understand the dynamics of this situation. Being an only child only serves to heighten my ignorance. But what I do know is that I am seeing utter joy and bliss in my boys as they share in this secret fraternity of brothers and fathers – something that I am not, nor will ever be, privy to. It is beyond my comprehension, and maybe that's just the way nature intended it.

Back to School

(to the tune of New York, New York – *with my sincere apologies to Frank Sinatra)*

Start spreadin' the news
Today is the day
I want to get there early
It's back to school!

Spent thousands on camp
They still said they're bored
I want to get there early
It's back to school!

They've fought for three months
We've screamed like white trash
I want to get there early
It's back to school!

I want to wake them
Before the sun hits the sky
And shove them onto the bus
Into the car
Out of the door
Out of my hair

My stay home mom blues
Are endin' today
I want to get there early
It's back to school!

If I can take them there
I can go anywhere
Oh happy day
It's back to school! Back to school!

Now I know that Christmas gets top billing as the most wonderful time – there's even a song about it. But whoever penned that ditty was obviously not a stay-at-home mother. On the Mom Calendar, the most magnificent time of year and cause for joyous celebration is, of course, the First Day of School.

Mere seconds after picking The Boys up on the last day of school things were already going to pot. Before I could even pull away from the curb, the fighting began. "MAKE HIM STOP!" Younger Boy screamed at a windshield shattering volume. "HE STARTED IT!" Older Boy shrieked back, blistering my eardrums. The moment we walked in the house, precisely 27 minutes into summer vacation, I was Googling year-round Swiss boarding schools.

By the end of June, the 24/7 togetherness was getting to me and I was ready to pull my hair out. "What can I do, I'm *soooo bored,*" Older Boy complained in a tone that sounded like a Valley Girl. "There's nothing cool to do," they whined in unison. "Go outside and play," I suggested helpfully. My mother's eyes would roll back in her head as she chanted this phrase like a mantra every day of summer vacation. Of course, I now understand this is Motherspeak for Go Away, You're Driving Me Crazy.

By July, they managed to negotiate a truce sensing they were stuck with each other for the duration. Although the peace was undoubtedly pleasant, the constant mess in every corner of the house and even the yard was maddening. Lego projects took over the kitchen table. The baking soda and vinegar volcano began to fossilize on the counter. A makeshift battleground complete with aircraft carriers and helicopters guarded the living room. Tents were erected in the backyard. My house had transformed into a real-life version of Bil Keane's *Family Circus*. And just like the cartoon, I had a trail of footprints leading everywhere The Boys had been.

But the hot, dry days at the end of the month caused a renegotiation of the truce and the fighting resumed with a furor. The battles were starting to take their toll on my mental health when a magical insert appeared in the Sunday newspaper – my beacon of hope - the first ad for a Back to School sale. The cavalry had arrived and visions of pencils and crayons and backpacks danced in my head. It wouldn't be long now. I clutched the ad to my chest until it was tattered from sweat, and quite possibly tears.

Optimism had returned, thanks to Kmart.

As the dog days of August seemed to grow longer, my patience grew shorter. After repeatedly banishing them to their rooms for their increasingly ridiculous skirmishes, you would think they'd figure it out by simple Tarzan process of elimination – FIGHTING BAD. Time seemed to literally stand still and I felt like Tom Hanks in *Cast Away* making hash marks of my remaining days marooned on Stay-At-Home-Isle. And just like Tom, I could often be found in my backyard hopelessly scanning the horizon, sweaty with a towel on my head, with HELP! scrawled in the dirt behind me.

But I focused my attention on that critical Wednesday circled in bright red, the First Day of School. "Time to go shopping for back to school," I announced trying to hide my unbridled glee. "Can't we wait another week?" Older Boy said. "I'm not ready yet."

Oh, but Mom is ready. And she's counting the days.

Worth A Thousand Words

"I thought you might want this," my mother said as she rooted through her enormous carry-on bag sitting on my kitchen table. She produced a cake box, which I hoped contained a slice, if not the whole carrot cake, from my favorite Louisville bakery. Upon closer inspection, the dented and dingy box looked like it might have been a vintage from my twelfth birthday. Not having the heart to turn down whatever it was she felt compelled to schlep through security and across the country for me, I tentatively flipped open the lid. Much to my disappointment, it wasn't cake.

It was a box of black and white photos. And some of the people in them looked an awful lot like me.

"These are your Grandma's pictures," my mother said. "I thought you might want to give them to The Boys someday."

I felt like I'd stumbled upon my own personal *Ancestry.com* stash. Here were the unsmiling, stoic faces representing my history, my roots. Excitedly, I flipped over the first photo of two kids sitting on a front porch to discover the names and places of my past.

And what did I learn? Absolutely nothing because the back of the picture was blank.

As was the next one, and the next one and the next one. Apparently my family had pretty crummy record keeping skills.

"Mom, there's NOTHING written on the back of these!" I whined. "Who are all of these people?"

Mom picked up pictures and rattled off names and places like an automatic weapon. "That's your Great Aunt Willadean at Oswald's house. There's Uncle Clevie. That's Denzil Ray at Modelle and Ozzie's wedding, because that's the only time he ever wore a suit."

Given the bizarre family names, I was starting to think that Uncle Frank Zappa, along with cousins Moon Unit and Dweezil might just show up in the next mug shot.

"How do you know all this?" I asked.

"Your Grandma told me," she replied matter-of-factly.

"Why didn't she write it down?" I demanded.

"Guess she never got around to it," Mom said. "Grandma didn't have to, she just knew."

I never got around to quizzing Mom so I could write down the names and places of each and every picture. And the ancient cake box of mystery history landed on the closet shelf next to my massive picture collection.

In a weekend fit of inspiration, I decided to organize my own family photos. I pulled out box after box randomly stuffed with twenty-two years worth of pictures of dogs, kids and road trips. I was sure I'd been a better record keeper than Grandma.

That is, until I pulled the first picture out.

There were two chocolate smeared toddlers at our rental house in New York, kneeling in front of a dented, harvest gold refrigerator in the kitchen we'd dubbed The Break Room due to the industrial-like quality of the linoleum. Smugly, I turned the photo over, remembering quite vividly the stay-at-home-mom moment of The Boys' cuteness in 1999. And what did I find?

Nothing. I hadn't written a word.

Apparently, I was a bad record keeper too. But I didn't have to write it down because like Grandma, I just knew.

So I'll probably never know about the people and places in the cake box of my past. And some day when The Boys are grown, I'll drop off a couple of cake boxes of my own unidentified photos to my two branches of the family tree. But I can up the ante. Because I'm throwing in Dad's mostly out-of-focus family vacation slides too.

What's In A Name?

Moments after discovering you are pregnant, you begin to comprehend the enormous responsibility that comes with that little bundle of dividing cells. Cribs, strollers, driving, dating and college tuition all scroll past on the mental screen. But one of the most important pre-birth tasks urgently awaits you - naming the baby. And while you're poring over baby name books and looking at websites one thing is for certain, you are probably going to make someone mad. Because Great Aunt Mildred is never going to understand why Mee Maw Bertha's name is not making your short list.

There are many things to consider when it comes to naming a child. Given that baby will be saddled with this moniker until old age, it's not a task to be taken lightly.

Some parents take a traditional approach with a wholesome, sturdy family name. What's easier than slapping a Junior or III on dad's name or going with an old-school grandparent name and calling it good? Some parents prefer tradition with a biblical twist choosing names like Matthew, Rachel or Methuselah.

Other families take a unique approach with trendy names. And nobody does it better than Celebrity Parents, because they can. I don't know if it's a testament to Star Parent hipness or if the true meaning is really less complicated: My Child Never Has To Seek Gainful Employment. You can bet Moon Unit, Dweezil and Diva Thin Pigeen Muffin Zappa have never written their names on any document that said Job Application at the top.

Not only will Sage Moonblood Stallone ever have to worry about getting a job, but he will never has to worry about getting teased. You don't have to when Rocky's your daddy.

While only the stars could pull off names like Buddy Bear (Jamie Oliver), Bear Blu (Alicia Silverstone), Diezel Ky (Toni Braxton) and Moxie Crimefighter (Penn Jillette), it still makes you wonder – what were they thinking? Makes the subject of the Johnny Cash song, "A Boy Named Sue," look downright normal.

Non-celebrity parents in New Zealand thought the name Talula Does the Hula From Hawaii was just swell for their baby girl. But thanks to the likes of Talula's eccentric parents, the crazy names are now subject to government scrutiny. So it should have come as no surprise when another New Zealand couple wanted to name their baby Lucifer, officials said hell no. Another couple settled on Superman when their original choice of 4Real was banned.

Like New Zealand, Sweden also takes a serious interest in baby names. So imagine the parents' surprise when their name Brfxxccmnpcccllllmnnprxvclmnckssqlbb1116 (pronounced Albin)

---

was declined. Metallica and Elvis were also banned, but Google and Lego received the thumbs up.

In this country, if your parents gave you any old boring name, don't despair. You have the right to change your handle to just about anything you can think of. Because why on earth would you want to be called Darren Lloyd Bean when your driver's license can read Darren QX (pronounced Lloyd) Bean! Think the name Peter Eastman, Jr. is a real snoozer? Why not call yourself Trout Fishing in America? And only in this great country of ours can a guy named Steve Kreuscher become In God We Trust.

But parents-to-be would be well advised to make sure baby naming is a joint venture. Because if you leave it up to your spouse, you might just end up with little ESPN (pronounced Espen) Montana Real. And that's exactly what Rusty and Leann Real of Mississippi did. But I think they missed their chance, nobody here would have batted an eye at 4Real.

Caught on Film

As Younger Boy closes out his elementary school career, it dawned on me that over the years I've attended nearly every single event for both my boys. Every play, every band concert, every choir performance. And don't forget the T-ball, soccer, baseball, cross country, track and taekwondo meets. It's not because I'm Super Mom; I've fully embraced my mediocrity as a parent – I'm a Real Mother. I've been there in Real Time alright, but I can't quite recall ever actually seeing anything. That's because I've viewed nearly every single important moment of their lives through the tiny viewfinder of my Sony Camcorder.

I've chronicled the first eleven years of Younger Boy's life on tape worthy of a multi-night Ken Burns PBS documentary. I've captured everything from his first wobbly steps to those once unsteady feet breaking boards at his most recent red belt test in taekwondo. I have footage of charming kindergarten plays involving rabbit ears. I have video of songs performed in first grade with that adorable enunciation that only two missing front teeth can provide. I have film of him playing the trombone with sounds effects like something from NASCAR. I have several cassettes that document nothing more than the rows of parents' heads seated in front of me.

In fact, it all makes me a little misty-eyed.

But that's probably just from chronic eyestrain after thirteen years of watching the high points of my children's lives through a half-inch square.

Funny thing is I've never watched a single one of my Spielberg-like masterpieces. The tape usually runs out, most often mid-performance, and is thrown in a box on the top shelf of my closet. And there they sit for posterity.

My mother has joined me in the quest to film every possible waking (and in the early years, sleeping) moment of her grandchildren's lives. The second I learned I was pregnant; my mother purchased video equipment in anticipation of her first grandchild. Unlike my grandpa's relatively small Super 8 from the 1960s that shot actual film with a grainy, strobe light quality, Mom's enormous cinematic set-up is probably what Mel Brooks used to film *Blazing Saddles*. Her first video cam was so big it used full size VHS tapes and came with a back brace.

Since my mother is a long-distance grandma, she actually watches her footage. And I suspect she cons her grandma friends into watching them too under the guise of stopping by for coffee. I'm betting she'd have a more enthusiastic crowd if she served gin and tonics.

So I considered it thoughtful when Mom made copies of

tapes from each baby's first year for me. That is, until I actually watched them. Mom's videos would send Alfred Hitchcock screaming from the room. They all start with her signature opening sequence– footage of her SAS shoes and her saying "Is this thing on?" When she suddenly realizes it's recording, the camera whips straight up and you've just strapped in for a spin on the Granny Cam Express. Her heart-stopping camera work reminds me of the *Blair Witch Project* or an episode of *COPS,* which leaves you begging for a seatbelt and a Dramamine. And then there's her narration which always seems to follow the same running dialogue. "Ronnie, look at him. Isn't he the cutest thing? That's nanny's cute boy! Yes him is! RONNIE, ARE YOU LOOKING AT HIM? ISN'T HE CUTE? RONNIE, ARE YOU LISTENING TO ME?"

So perhaps one day, I'll sit down and watch the hours of film I've taken. But if my videos turn out anything like my mother's, there's a good chance I'll need a neckbrace. And a gin and tonic.

Full Moon Lunacy

"Don't make me get out of this sleeping bag," a voice hissed in the dark.

Instead, the giggles grew louder. Pretty soon, the laughter became uncontrolled. It bordered on lunacy, which was appropriate given the blinding full moon illuminating the tent.

"I'm not kidding," he said. "If I get out, we are leaving."

The next think I knew, a flashlight was blinding me. Eight-year-old Older Boy stood over The Husband and me like a short, angry detective looking for a confession.

"You two have to stop laughing," he said. "No one can sleep."

Right on cue, Younger Boy snored in the background.

Older Boy shrugged, pulled his toboggan down over his face and crawled headfirst into the bag.

I had reached the cackle stage best characterized by snorts, tears and difficulty breathing. And it was a good thing. Because if I wasn't laughing, I would've been crying.

I was not a happy camper.

Once upon a time, The Husband and I were contented backpackers. We could throw together a weeklong camping trip in our external frame packs in a few short hours and disappear. We had an A-frame North Face two-person tent with fat plastic stakes. Water boiled on our Optimus stove that weighed in at about a pound and a half. And that worked just fine.

Until we had kids.

Suddenly life was a whole lot more complicated and sleep deprived. If there was a remote chance I could sleep I wanted it to be on my Serta, not a Thermarest that wheezed with my every move. The thought of putting together a camping trip with kids and dogs began to sound more like assembling the supplies for an extended Himalayan trek, except with more gear. So we gave up camping in the great outdoors and our now dated, heavy gear gathered dust on a shelf in the garage.

Roughing it became a motel that didn't serve a complimentary hot breakfast.

But when I saw the smiling family of four sitting in a pristine campsite on the tent box at Costco, I couldn't resist bringing it home. Because they looked like happy campers. The tent, which was bigger than my first apartment, claimed to be easy to assemble, practically set up with a mere flick of the wrist.

Sucker.

After 45 minutes of watching of our efforts collapse in a heap, The Husband and I stood on top of what was supposed to be our tent, arguing.

"The pole goes THIS way," I said as if the mere tone of my voice would force it into place. "No, it goes THIS way," The Husband countered. Having heard enough, eight-year-old Older Boy walked over, took the poles from our hands and snapped them into place with a flick of his wrist. He rolled his eyes and went back to looking for bugs under rocks.

That's when I discovered I only brought two sleeping bags. "The kids can use the sleeping bags," The Husband announced. "You and I can use the dog blankets."

So as I shivered wide-awake on my asthmatic Thermarest trying my best not to aspirate another tuft of dog fur, I began to giggle. At that precise moment, every occupant of the adjoining campsite began to shuffle off to the potty with footfalls so precise, I thought it might be the members of Riverdance breaking into an impromptu performance by the light of the full moon. By that time, The Husband joined me in a fit of laughter. And that's exactly when Older Boy reprimanded us with the threat of leaving.

And I would have been delighted to go – but only where there's room service.

Udderly Ridiculous

I scream, you scream, we all scream for ice cream. But if the People for the Ethical Treatment of Animals (PETA) has its way – it's None for Me, Thanks.

PETA officials sent a letter to Ben Cohen and Jerry Greenfield, the creators of Ben & Jerry's Ice Cream, urging them to replace cow's milk in their divine creations with human breast milk.

Am I the only one out there who visibly wretched at this idea?

I think most people would wholeheartedly agree that breast is best. For babies, yes, not frozen confectionary treats. Even the La Leche folks were left scratching their heads at this off-the-wall suggestion. But PETA based this nutty notion on Storchen, a Swiss restaurant, whose menu includes soups, stews and sauces made with 75% human breast milk. With the exception of perhaps Russ Meyer, I'm betting most adults who are decades beyond the breast feeding years would unequivocally concur that this is, well, gross.

And what would become of my beloved Ben & Jerry products? Would there be Peanut Butter C Cup? Hooter Crunch? Coffee with Cream? Mammary Mint Chip? Would Baskin Robbins follow suit and become 32 D Flavors?

I shudder at the thought.

PETA Executive Director Tracy Reiman suggested that "using breast milk would reduce the suffering of cows." While that may be true, I wonder who Ms. Reiman thinks will be bellying up to the pumping station. Worn out new mothers, that's who. This proposition would put exhausted new mothers to work in the equivalent of an ice cream sweatshop. Moo-ve over Bessy, punch out and rest. Momma's here.

I'm just speculating that Ms. Reiman has not fallen asleep with her head on the kitchen counter and her robe on backwards after an exhausted night of nursing her new baby every two hours. I'm also guessing she never toted a breast pump to the office and tried to return phone calls over the din of the groaning machine. "What? What's that noise? Construction. Outside my window." Asking new mothers to pull double shift to let a few cows off the hook borders on cruel and unusual.

Isn't our country's pathetic maternity leave punishment enough?

But there might just be a silver lining, at least for lactating Montana women. Because all women know the real reason we breast feed. Sorry ladies, I'm about to blow our cover. Every woman chooses to become a 24/7 human buffet line for one reason only – to get out of jury duty.

At least one Montana lawmaker thinks so.

Speaking against a bill to excuse nursing mothers from their civic duty, lawmaker Keith Regier's comment indicated that he had cracked the vast statewide lactation conspiracy wide open. "This looks like an easy-out for a parent," he concluded.

By golly Keith, you're on to us.

Perhaps Keith and the Judge who refused to excuse a new mom from jury service would feel differently if Momma was also working the 4 o'clock shift at Ben & Jerry's. I can just imagine that courtroom exchange.

"Your Honor, I'm a nursing mother, may I please be excused?"

"If I let you out for something trivial like that, I'd just have to excuse everyone, wouldn't I?

"Your Honor, I have to be at work at Ben & Jerry's by 4."

"A working mother? Why didn't you say so? EXCUSED!"

For me, it's difficult to say which idea is wackier – putting breast milk in ice cream or not excusing nursing mothers from jury duty. Because the way I see it, they are both udderly ridiculous.

Oh Baby!

Michelle Duggar, 41, recently announced that she and hubby Jim Bob were expecting baby number eighteen. As a card-carrying member of the motherhood sorority, I am deeply humbled. Michelle, you have taken this Baby Momma gig to new and unprecedented heights and we women with mere mortal reproductive systems are not worthy. As the mother of two, my hat is off to you.

I was pretty tickled with two since round one of pregnancy and delivery was enough to make me wave the white flag in complete surrender. After 36 hours of no drugs allowed labor followed by a dramatic emergency C-section, I was pretty proud of myself for even considering number two, much less getting back on the proverbial pregnancy horse. But not wanting to follow in the ever-fertile footsteps of my great-grandmothers, Gertie, who had 10 and Mary, who threw a litter of 14, I took matters into my own hands. After my second C-section, I wanted my tubes tied – and don't forget the double knots. I wanted no chance of a round three.

But after spending only 18 short months of my life pregnant, I have to admit, there's some morbid curiosity about what it might be like to spend 11 full YEARS of your life knocked up. Considering that the average fifth grader understands the mechanics of the pregnancy thing, I just can't imagine Michelle waking up pregnant with number 12 saying, "Well dang, Jim Bob, how'd *that* happen again?" It's quite clear, Fertile Myrtle, it's time to get proactive. Cross your legs. Get a patch. Fake a headache.

The *Brady Bunch*, *Eight is Enough* and *Yours, Mine and Ours*, while cutesy, make me shudder with fear at the thought of living in a house with the population of a small town in Wyoming. Seeing the photo of Michelle and Jim Bob surrounded by their growing brood of fresh faced kiddos ranging in age from 20 years down to 19 months made me want to remove my own reproductive organs with a rusty chain saw, just in case.

I can only imagine poor Michelle's uterus cringing when newly united sperm and egg number nineteen come cruising down the fallopian tube highway looking for a parking space. I bet that over-worked womb wants to hold up a sign like Wyle E. Coyote after being smashed under a giant anvil that sums it up in one word – *HELP!*

I have to admit, I thought it was sheer brilliance to divide up the housework into jurisdictions making each child responsible for some segment of household chores and maintenance. That alone would be enough for me to consider adding a few extra to the line-up so I don't have to dust, vacuum and clean the toilet. But I decided it would be much wiser, and probably cheaper, to just call Merry

Maids.

I suspect the real motive behind this fertility machine is that Jim Bob, a former member of the Arkansas Legislature, wants to revisit his unsuccessful U.S. Senate candidacy by single handedly creating his own voting district. If you want to win the election, Jim Bob, give the little woman a break and get out there and maybe just kiss a few babies instead of making them.

If your intention is garnering the national media spotlight, I'd say you've got that covered. You've made appearances on everything from *Discovery* to *CNN* and have your own Unreality Show. The blessed event of upcoming baby eighteen was announced during a live spot on the *Today Show*. If an appearance on *Oprah* is your ultimate goal, I bet Eighteen is Enough.

Like the seventeen siblings that came before him or her, baby eighteen will have a name beginning with "J." You can actually vote online at *DiscoveryHealth.com* for your favorite. But I'm going to write in my pick: Junta. Because after popping out eighteen babies, Momma Michelle should stage a coup.

Lucky 13

Older Boy will turn fourteen in the near future and I'm planning a blowout to mark this auspicious occasion. I do love birthdays but this year it's just a little different. This year I'm going to celebrate not killing him while he was thirteen.

Call me a sentimental fool.

As much as I hate to admit, it's not entirely his fault. Responsibility for this rests elsewhere. Because when things go wrong in my life, there's only one person to blame - my mother.

This whole predicament falls squarely on her shoulders and I'm betting she'd freely admit it.

Because it all started when I was thirteen.

When I was thirteen, I knew EVERYTHING. And I let my parents know that I had now acquired a superior intellect upon my recent entry into the teenage years and that I really didn't need their advice anymore. I could handle life on my own now, *thankyouverymuch*, despite the fact I was in 8th grade, unemployed and without a driver's license.

I was also fairly certain that my parents had transformed into the dumbest people on planet Earth. I was confident that their sole purpose in life was to embarrass their only daughter. And I made it a point to let them know this at every possible waking moment.

As my mother would say, "She's got a mouth on her that won't quit."

My mother, being a woman of infinite patience, tried to talk to me. I would just give her a dramatic eye roll, sigh and start mouthing off about one of her stupid, mom-like ideas. After awhile, she began to ignore my disparaging adolescent remarks. But one day, my mother simply had enough of my teenage outbursts and know-it-all attitude.

And that's when it happened.

Having been the recipient of one too many theatrical eye rolls, coupled with a startling "MOM!" pronounced as three syllables and my harsh, unrelenting teenage criticisms, my mother was rightfully at wit's end.

And she lost it.

With that, my mother did the only thing she could think of: she put the Voodoo Whammy Curse on me. Before the next hateful word could fall from my lips, she stuck her index finger an inch from my nose, looked me right in the eye and said through gritted teeth, "One day, you'll have a kid who talks to you just like you're talking to me." She then turned on her heel and left the room.

I can still hear her laughing.

Before the words could evaporate from the air, they banded

together and with a whoosh, landed somewhere in my right ovary where they glommed onto the tiny cell that would become half of Older Boy. At that moment, my know-it-all thirteen-year-old brain could not contemplate the power of The Curse. In fact, I promptly forgot about it for the next thirty-four years until the day Older Boy turned thirteen. Within forty-seven seconds of the clock ushering in his teenage years, Older Boy had a mouth on him that wouldn't quit. Just like his mother.

The Voodoo Whammy Curse had worked.

Of course, I called mom to share the news and she was rendered speechless. Mainly because she was laughing too hard to speak.

But now with Younger Boy in middle school too, I'm going to have to call her again. Mom, I don't know if you planned on hitting a double with The Curse. But rest assured you hit the first one out of the park, so I get it. Please, remove The Curse before Younger Boy becomes a teenager.

I'm begging you.

Reality Check

I recently saw a commercial advertising the upcoming episode of the latest version of *Survivor* playing out on some far off tropical isle. As I watched their struggles and conflicts during the thirty-second sound bite, I just chuckled. Another commercial followed depicting a woman's face, contorted in horror, as she was about to do the unthinkable – bob for a pig's tongue in a vat of animal fat - for the chance at a million bucks.

Please, challenge me.

Why so smug? Am I a slighted, past *Survivor* show participant, unfairly voted off the island early? No, but I know all about survival. I am a member of the tribe of original survivors: I'm a stay-at–home mom.

Being dropped on Vanuatu or in the Australian Outback sounds like a vacation compared to my daily life as a mom with two kids under the age of two. I am the Weakest Link. There are days I wish Donald Trump would knock on my door and announce,

"You're fired!" I might stop to give him a hug as I ran out the door. Voluntarily having raw sewage poured on your head pales in comparison to the Fear Factor of fishing a hysterical toddler's toy from the bottom of poop filled potty before you've even had your morning coffee.

Until I traded my briefcase for a diaper bag, I never realized how much work was involved in the daily life of being home with kids. I am living my own version of the Surreal Life, now having no memory of my life before children. Getting two kids up, dressed, fed, and out of the house before noon is my own Amazing Race.

And that's an easy day.

This does not include the days with tantrums, teething, and assorted ear infections that turn Days into Nightmares that can bring a grown woman to her knees. By the end of those days I look just like a reality show contestant clad in filthy, mismatched clothes: sweaty, dirty and somewhat wild-eyed from sleep deprivation. During those moments, I would probably be eligible for the only two reality shows that would ever even consider me: *What Not to Wear* and *Extreme Makeover*.

I propose a new reality show that will actually be based in reality. My show - "Survivor – The Suburbs – The Two Under Two Challenge." In my version, the premise is simple: the individual contestants are dropped in craftsman bungalows in the suburbs, located at least one mile from another house with a stay-at-home parent. The contestants are in charge of two children, ages six weeks and seventeen months.

All day. Every day. With no help from others for one full

year.

At the start of the series, a minivan full of supplies is placed in the driveway along with the children who are strapped in their car seats. The contestants are then given five minutes to salvage what supplies they can from the cargo area of a minivan while carrying the two children into the house. Contestants can't be voted out and they can't voluntarily leave. The lone survivor wins $122,732, the estimated worth of services performed by a stay-at-home mom for a year.

The Challenges will be as follows:

Episode 1: Diaper Wars: It's 10:30 p.m. and you have used the last disposable diaper.

Episode 2: Growing pains: Seventeen month old is teething, baby is colicky.

Episode 3: Under siege: Stomach flu takes over the house.

Episode 4: Wake up call: The children wake up at 4:30 a.m. daily.

Episode 5: Just say *ah*: Checkup time for the children, complete with immunizations.

Episode 6: Ear ecstasy: Oldest child receives a Band in a Box toy from Grandma complete with cymbals, tambourine and maracas.

Episode 7: Take aim: Potty training and the surprising world of bodily function.

Episode 8: Trouble in Paradise: A week in Hawaii with the in-laws following the 8 hour flight to get there.

Special two hour season finale: It's My Party (and I'll cry if I want to): Throw a birthday party complete with clowns and a petting zoo for the oldest child and ten of his closest friends.

The overall winner will be chosen from a panel of 5.4 million parenting experts – the army of stay-at-home moms across the nation who are in the trenches every single day.

Step off, Simon.

And just like the rest of us, the winner's grand prize of $122,732 will be payable in peanut butter and jelly kisses; cards made from glue, glitter and elbow macaroni; and spontaneous "I love yous" that make you feel like a true American Idol.

Who's willing to Outwit, Outplay and Outlast now?

Parenting Like Tony

Hard for me to believe, but this spring my baby finished elementary school. After eight years (he's no Jethro; I had two kids go to that school) of walking those comforting halls with the faint aroma of crayons and pencils and second-home to some of the best teachers on the planet, I never have a reason to go there again. Although I've never been a Dwell in the Past Person, it made me just a little wistful. So what's a mom to do when her youngest is about to join his brother in middle school?

Embarrass the hell out of him, of course.

Because when I was pregnant, I operated under the delusion that I would be Super Mom. In my maternal daydreams I'd be wearing something purple and gauzy while speaking in reassuring, yet authoritative, tones to my wee-one sitting at my feet. "And darling, that is why the sky is blue," I'd explain. Of course, my perfect child would gaze lovingly into my eyes and say, "Oh yes, mother dear, I do understand. Now can we go pick the organic apples that we've grown so we can make applesauce together?"

Clearly I was hormonally insane.

After being in the trenches of child rearing, I realize that my parenting bears no resemblance whatsoever to my Beloved Earth Mother Fantasy. My approach to raising kids is nothing like Dr. Spock espoused. I'm no Super Nanny either. In reality, I parent more like Tony Soprano using bribery, coercion and threats. And I bet Tony would tell me that threats are only as good as your ability to back them up.

So when a member of the planning committee approached me to do a project for the fifth grade send off, I was surprised. "We'd like you to write a funny song," she said.

Me? Write a song? I will happily sing (badly) any number from *Hairspray, Chicago* or *Jesus Christ Superstar*, but this in no way qualifies me to pen a musical score. Composing music requires a working knowledge of melodic overtones. It requires a thorough understanding of diatonic modes and rhythm. It, in short, requires talent.

But after careful consideration, I decided it would be the perfect vehicle for my nefarious parenting purposes. I couldn't write a song, but I could write a rap, which as Vanilla Ice so vividly demonstrated, requires no talent whatsoever. So I agreed on one condition, that it be a total surprise.

On the last day of school, a gang of extremely enthusiastic fifth grade moms joined me to perform my little rap to bid adieu to our children's years in elementary school.

And in my humble opinion, we rocked the house.

There was only one thing funnier than the horrified looks of utter embarrassment on our kids' faces as we strutted our stuff on stage: the faces of our significant others. Shocking Younger Boy was one thing, but seeing The Husband's jaw smack the floor was simply a bonus.

As Younger Boy heads off to middle school with his brother, I'd like him to take along this little message. Just like Santa, I know if you've been naughty or nice. And if you're in trouble, your most feared words in the English language will no longer be, "Wait Till your Father Gets Home." Instead the words that will invoke maximum anxiety are now, "School Assembly." Because if you've been bad, it just might be the Revenge of Momma D and her Rapper Mom Posse.

So yo, yo my little Home Boys, don't mess with Momma D. Because she can embarrass you. And now you know for sure, she will.

I think Tony would be proud.

Baby Talk at 49

I was in pain. A LOT of pain. My abdomen felt like the creature from *Alien* might come busting out with a cinematic flourish. I hadn't been in that much pain since I went into spasmodic back labor while unsuccessfully attempting to deliver Older Boy nearly fifteen years ago. Now I felt so wretched, I tried those breathing exercises from prenatal class. And once again, they were pretty much useless.

The pain wasn't improving. As I writhed in misery, The Husband announced, "We're going to the emergency room."

A short while later, I was lying on a gurney having enough blood removed from my dehydrated and collapsing veins to qualify as a character in an Anne Rice novel. My stomach was poked, prodded and not surprisingly deemed soft. As The Husband answered questions, a kind nurse told me relief was on the way. There was a rush and then the pain slowly drifted away. I felt almost human again. Then I feel asleep.

Then the physician's assistant came in so quietly that I barely heard her. "We need to talk about a few things," I heard her say through my pharmaceutical fog. I was expecting something like, "Your appendix is the size of New Jersey." Or perhaps, "Your spleen exploded." But nothing prepared me for the words she spoke. "We should do a pregnancy test."

As you might suspect, this woman had my undivided attention.

"That's n-not possible," I stammered, completely awake now. "I'm two weeks away from my 49th birthday. I have an AARP card in my wallet! And most importantly, I've been fixed!"

"Sometimes a tubal can fail," she continued calmly.

"Failure is not an option," I told her channeling my best Apollo 13 Command Center voice. I was thankful The Husband had not been in the room. Otherwise, we'd be sharing His & Hers Gurneys while waiting for the cardiac team to revive him.

"Look," I argued pointing at my belly. "This baguette of flesh below my navel is a menopot, not a baby bump. I know in one of my favorite, extremely unflattering shirts people might think I *look* pregnant. But my eggs aren't looking to hook up, they're asking for directions to the senior center."

She smiled and stood up. "I'll let you know." With a quick mental calculation, I realized by the time I was finished feeding Baby applesauce and changing diapers that Baby would be changing mine. When Baby graduated high school, The Husband would be 70. At that point, not only was I contemplating breaking the hospital rule of turning on my cell phone, I was ready to call Dr. Kevorkian on it.

Then I remembered my colleague when I was pregnant with Younger Boy. My middle-aged friend thought she was menopausal. Instead, she was preggers at 48. We delivered within weeks of each other.

I drifted back into my pain med haze where I vacillated between dreaming about the not-so-far-off empty nest and pink footie pajamas. I wondered if stretch marks could get stretch marks. By the time I fell back asleep, I had picked out names.

Before I could contemplate the merits of baby slings, the PA returned. "You're not pregnant," she said. I made her say it three times then write it down in really big letters so I could see it without my glasses, just to be sure.

So I guess feathering the nest with one more, while shocking, would have been just fine. But I would have been one tired old bird.

That's No Baby, That's a Mid-Life Crisis

First of all, I'd like to say a Big Thank You to my kind readers and friends who e-mailed, brought me flowers and stopped to me to ask, "Was it just gas?" once I was finally walking upright. Big Hugs to all of you. The mystery ailment was solved by my wise doctor after the ER folks thoroughly ruled out an exploding spleen along with organs I didn't even know I had. My doctor handed me a sheet listing the symptoms of an extremely nasty viral diagnosis. And I could place a check mark by each and every one of them except the one I would have actually welcomed – weight loss.

So I should be celebrating the fact that I'm physically OK. But I'm not. That's because tomorrow I'll be celebrating something else – my birthday. And I'm not feeling all that festive. Because it's the last one of the 40s.

I smell a midlife crisis.

In 1983, Karen Kavet wrote a book called "I'd Rather Be 40 Than Pregnant." I hear ya, sister. But way back then, I was fresh out of college. Being pregnant, not to mention impossibly old like my 43-year-old mother, seemed an eternity away. Now I fully understand Kavet's sentiments. But after the Great Emergency Room Pregnancy Scare of 2010, as it will be forever known in our family lore, I'll up the ante. Because honey, I think I'd rather be 50 than pregnant.

So I suppose there is a silver lining even with a midlife crisis on the horizon.

But this household has already survived one. Being the elder statesman of the Family Unit, The Husband has weathered the midlife crisis storm. And let me tell you, he cruised right through Manopause – on a Harley. Actually he kind of sailed through it too after his Captain Ahab death on the High Seas phase of piloting a sailboat in a circle at Canyon Ferry. And let's not forget the brief, yet ear splitting, late-40s Rock Star moment of playing the drums.

And The Boys laughed and laughed at their dad.

But it could have been a lot worse. The Husband could have pulled up in a shiny red BMW convertible, sporting a spray tan, a generous application of Just For Men and tacky gold chains. At which point I would've become a widow. Because I would have had to kill him for looking so totally ridiculous.

Now I'm glad I didn't say a word because it's all going to slingshot right back at me. Here I sit contemplating the last year of my forties thinking I really should do something memorable to commemorate this upcoming major life passage. Should I take up rock climbing? Run a marathon? Try singing lessons? Finally write that book? Or maybe just finish reading one?

Do I put on my Big Girl Panties and embrace my true age and the Wisdom of Menopause? Or do I head into this battle with a chemically enhanced face incapable of expressing basic human emotions, liposuctioned thighs and a brand new pair of silicone doorknobs?

I just don't know. But what I do know is The Boys will be laughing at me.

But a long, long time from now, The Boys will be middle-aged men facing a midlife crisis of their very own. And like their parents before them, they'll muddle through. But no matter what The Old Boys do, I take comfort in one fact: knowing their kids will be laughing at them.

Flashback to Jingle Hell

I didn't need to consult Albert Einstein to know traveling back in time is possible. All it took was a visit to the Target restroom while Christmas shopping. And it was 1999 all over again.

When I entered this time portal, I saw a harried mom, a cart shoved in the corner corralling two rowdy toddlers and one closed stall door. "Hurry please," the mom begged the third child behind the door. I flashed the Mom Gang Sign to let her know Been There, Done That, This Too Shall Pass. I think she would've appreciated a double martini more.

Then I promptly experienced a flashback to my own trip to Jingle Hell.

It was three days before Christmas. I was filling the cart for a massive holiday feast. I was trying to accomplish this feat before picking up the Parental Unit at the airport on a day I'd planned with the efficiency of a time-motion expert - with a 3-year-old and a 1-year-old in tow.

Against the odds, I triumphantly rounded the corner to the checkout like Zenyata at the Breeder's Cup. That's when Older Boy said, "Mommy, me go potty." This unscheduled pit stop was not part of the plan. "It's OK if you go in your Pull Up," I said dashing to the shortest line that was backed up into the health and beauty aisle.

Older Boy furrowed his brow considering my proposition. Younger Boy had grown bored and began throwing his blankie out of the cart for a rousing game of Mommy Fetch.

The line didn't budge.

In a voice that could be heard from deli to produce, Older Boy announced, "Mommy, me go poopy. NOW!"

Alrighty then.

Relinquishing my place in line, I sprinted to the restroom. Normally I'd just shove the cart right in the door to contain Younger Boy until I saw the sign "No Unpaid Merchandise Beyond This Point."

Parking the cart, I shouted, "I'll be right back," to no one in particular. With a kid under each arm, I dashed in to thankfully find one open stall. Putting Older Boy down, I began papering the seat while balancing Younger Boy on my hip with the dexterity of a circus performer. "Don't touch anything!" I hissed because all germ-covered surfaces in a public restroom immediately become kids magnets for an unrestrained toddler.

Squatting next to the toilet, I tried to balance Older Boy on the unstable inch of paper while keeping a firm grasp on wiggly Younger Boy. Deciding adventure was elsewhere, Younger Boy

---

broke free. I cringed as his tiny hands hit the floor, which I imagined as a vile Petri dish cocktail. Seeing the shoes in the next stall, he beelined to make a new friend. Grabbing his feet while keeping Older Boy precariously on his perch, I contorted like Cirque du Mom within the confines of the stall. "Hi!" Younger Boy chirped poking his head into the next stall. "HI! HI! HI!" His new friend was not amused.

"Santa will bring you a Tickle Me Elmo if you hurry up," I told Older Boy as the sweat began to run down my forehead. "HI! HI! HI!" Younger Boy chanted as I pulled him back into our stall. "PLEASE HURRY; MAYBE SANTA WILL BRING YOU A CAR," I pleaded.

Satisfied that I'd upped the ante, Older Boy looked pleased. "Done," he said, "Just a little smoke came out."

I'm happy to report that Tickle Me Elmo appeared under the tree as promised. But if Santa brought anyone a car after that ordeal, it better have been for me.

Yeah, I Speak Thumb

Just when I got used to listening to yakasses on their cell phones revealing their innermost secrets to everyone within earshot in Target, mysteriously their voices went silent. After careful observation, I determined that folks continued to communicate with their phones, but much to my disappointment, I was no longer privy to their public, one-sided discussions. People were still talking – with their thumbs.

I've watched texting teens work those tiny cell phone keyboards using only their opposable thumbs faster than I could operate an IBM Selectric with all 10 digits after an entire year in Mrs. Smother's 10th-grade typing class. And it's no surprise these young masters of linguistic minimalism can pack so much into a few quick keystrokes, because from what I can tell, they're not even speaking English.

They're speaking thumb.

In the language of thumb, there's no need to worry about

subject/verb agreement. Irregular verbs? Forget about it. In fact, while communicating in thumb, real words are strictly optional.

So now I understand why my attempts at texting have been so incredibly frustrating. While I could get away with signing a school yearbook with "2 good 2 B 4-gotten," under no circumstances was I ever allowed to butcher grammar or spelling in Mrs. Steven's seventh-grade English class. I've been foolishly trying to text in the English language, with complete sentences and proper spelling like she drilled into my adolescent brain so long ago. If she were still teaching today, Mrs. Stevens would be standing at the chalkboard diagramming a road map of the linguistic horror that occurs when you let your participle dangle. No doubt, at that very moment in the back of the classroom, a yawning student would be tapping this succinct message into her hidden cell phone – "TIR BRD" (teacher in room, bored).

It's enough to make you LOL.

While one of the problems of texting is the destruction of the English language as we know it, the other fairly soon-to–be quandary is an anatomical one. That's right, big physical changes are on the way and we don't need to consult Mr. Darwin to see where this is headed. If you've ever observed a herd of teens walking around the mall, eyes glazed over while glued to their cell phone screens and thumbs typing away, you know exactly what I mean. Next up on the evolution menu are freakishly over-sized phalanges, that's what. With 2.5 billion texts circulating the United States each day, we're going to have thumbs the size of turkey legs.

And that's not the only physical change that will take place.

Since thanks to texting, actual speaking will no longer be necessary to convey thoughts, our vocal chords will shrivel from lack of use. Any essential communication that can't be achieved via thumb-speak will revert to the simplicity of caveman-like grunting and pointing. Because why engage in face-to-face human contact when you can key it in? Our eyeballs won't yet go the way of cave dwelling fish because we'll need them to be functional enough to read incoming messages. But we'll all be so near-sighted from staring at these miniature screens and keyboards, we'll be covered in bruises from walking into walls. Our remaining digits will morph into a marsupial cell phone pouch where our fingers used to be.

This isn't going to be a good look, people.

But I'm going to jump on the texting bandwagon anyway. And I think I'll be a natural. Because when it comes to technology, I'm all thumbs.

It Worked For Woodward and Bernstein

I can't believe this column isn't the front page, above the fold, lead story today. Because this is Breaking News. I thought I'd stumbled upon the Watergate story of the Parenting World, complete with an anonymous source. But there are no break-ins, wiretaps or tapes. There is no cloak and dagger-style espionage or late night meetings in semi-dark parking garages where my informant is wearing dark glasses and a trench coat. It was simply through solid investigative journalism that I cracked this story wide open.

In the spirit of Woodward and Bernstein, I will protect my confidential source. You can subpoena me, make me pay fines or throw me in jail like Judith Miller.

Because I'm not talking.

I will tell you that I call my secret informant Smart Girl. And that won't narrow it down one bit. Because as far as I can tell, there are a whole lot of them in this valley.

While I will not reveal her identity, I will share the intel I obtained on that fateful cloudy day. It was so shocking, as a member of the Parenting Tribe, I knew this information could not be dispensed on a need to know basis. Because parents You. Need. To. Know.

Smart Girl told me Middle Schoolers are Going Out. That's right, they're dating.

Sensing this story was Big News, I remained objective as a good reporter should and asked a well-reasoned line of probing questions. "WHAT DO YOU MEAN THEY ARE GOING OUT?" I shrieked hysterically. "YOU ALL ARE TWELVE AND THIRTEEN YEARS OLD. NONE OF YOU CAN EVEN DRIVE YET! WHERE ARE YOU GOING AND, MORE IMPORTANTLY, HOW ARE YOU GETTING THERE?"

I'm glad I was driving so I couldn't see her roll her eyes.

Without giving Smart Girl time to answer, I continued my careful inquiry. "HOW LONG HAS THIS BEEN GOING ON?" I screeched at a windshield rattling volume. "AND BE STRAIGHT WITH ME, IS MY KID GOING OUT?"

That was about the time that Mango Melon SoBe hit the windshield. Smart Girl was laughing so hard it shot out her nose.

When she regained her composure, Smart Girl asked me, "What do *you* think Going Out means?"

"It means that you Go Somewhere, like to dinner and a movie," I replied. "You know, like a date."

Smart Girl remained remarkably poised although it was clear she was trying hard not to spray the windshield with SoBe again.

But she continued. "It's not like that at all," she explained.

"YOU HAVE TO TELL ME," I loudly blathered on, "WHAT DOES IT MEAN?"

Thanks to my line of razor-sharp questioning, I had her exactly where I wanted her. "It means they sit together at lunch and don't talk to each other," she said matter-of-factly. I can't confirm or deny this but I'm pretty sure there was another eye roll at this juncture.

So nothing has changed since I was in 7th grade.

Except when I was in junior high, there was one boy who really could have gone out. Elvis Ray James flunked 7th grade so many times by the time I landed there he had already voted in a presidential election. He routinely inquired when they were adding a student parking lot.

Elvis Ray was every mother's worst nightmare.

So on that day with Smart Girl, I'm glad I didn't overreact. It was a relief to learn that the Middle School version of Going Out story wasn't even worthy of the National Enquirer. But I remain on Red Alert for the Next Big Story. You never know where Elvis is going to turn up.

Hormonal Insanity in the Land of Perfect Motherhood

When I was pregnant, I knew exactly what life was going to be like with my new bundle of joy. I envisioned it as a daily state of Nirvana-like, maternal ecstasy. I imagined blissfully strolling out to my newly planted organic garden with baby in my arms. I'd show my sweet, inquisitive child the bright green peas that I'd just picked, still misty with morning dew. In the house, I would gently mash them into homemade baby food, which he would eat before agreeably lying down for his afternoon nap.

Looks like a case of hormonal insanity.

Because from the moment I brought Older Boy home from the hospital, every day I feared I was somehow screwing him up.

The hormonal insanity of pregnancy was nothing compared to the complete madness I learned in the pages of parenting books in my quest for Child Rearing Perfection. Before Older Boy even arrived, I'd worked myself into a maternal frenzy based on what I'd read.

Yes, I drank the Kook-Aid in my attempt to join the Cult of the Perfect Mother.

I was going to get it right from diapers to dating. I was so desperate I even sought advice from the author of a parenting book who didn't even HAVE kids. But I had to know. Would I be an attachment parent? Would I Ferberize? Helicopter? Or simply drop from sheer mental exhaustion before baby even had the opportunity to deprive me of sleep?

By the time Older Boy actually made his appearance, two weeks late and in a spectacular display of Look Who's The Boss Now, I was in panic mode. Would I be a screen-free parent? Would I manage to be scream-free? An un-parent? Would I embrace elimination communication (diaperless parenting) and the notion that all of the flooring in my house would need to be ripped up and replaced with concrete, a drain and an industrial strength hose?

By the time Younger Boy came along, I had mellowed. Through trial and mostly error, I figured out one sure thing about parenting and myself: I was not, nor would I ever be the Perfect Mother. Because in reality, I found that trying to be the Perfect Mother was Perfect Madness. I didn't worry anymore when my house looked like the food fight scene in *Animal House* and needed a two-drink minimum sign on the front door. I stopped feeling guilty that they both could sing the *Gilligan's Island* theme song before they went to kindergarten. I quit worrying that my abs would forever be in protective custody. I gave in to the truth that some days Froot Loops were a food group. Armed with this knowledge, I had finally discovered my true parenting style – Slacker Mom. Sue me, I'm Real.

We were all much happier for it.

And then at the precise moment when I thought I might actually make it through the teenage years, a new parenting treatise came along. Tiger Mom, Amy Chua, turned up on the top of the food chain. According to Tiger Mom's agenda, if you're not roaring, you are Loser Parent, and worse you will have Loser Kid who will never, ever get into Harvard.

Mommie Weirdest, try some de-caf.

And that's just fine. Because when I returned from my journey to that mythical Land of Perfect Parenthood, I discovered that I already had the only thing I needed and that no book could ever teach: common sense.

The Verdict On Junk Food

Trouble was brewing in the cereal aisle. And the one about to incur the wrath was me. As my 'tween and teenaged sons stood there, it was clear they were about to make their case with the tenacity of Perry Mason and Atticus Finch. "See Mom, you were wrong!" Older Boy said shoving the box within an inch of my middle-aged eyes. "Go ahead, read it." Younger Boy then chimed in. "They're GOOD for you," he argued. "It says so right on the box."

My bad.

It was hard to argue with the good health claims emblazoned on the front of the Cocoa Krispies and Froot Loops boxes that my boys paraded in front of me like I was a Price is Right Showcase Contestant. There they were – boxes of an immunity-boosting, fiber enhanced morning indulgence that I've denied them based on my misguided beliefs. And boy did I feel pretty stupid. All these years I've been making them eat real froot.

Since they were little guys, I operated under the apparent delusion that spinach, broccoli and bananas were the building blocks for healthy bodies. Silly me. Looks like I could have saved a bundle at the pediatrician's office if I'd been offering them those little orbs of crunchy chocolate goodness from the time they sprouted choppers. I probably could have by-passed all those annoying vaccinations if I'd jammed enough of it down their young pie holes.

So that got me thinking, why couldn't we take better living through chemistry a step further with the marriage of junk food and pharmaceuticals? It wouldn't even be a shotgun wedding. Seems the government fat cats anticipated this day would come when they created the bureaucracy known as the Food and Drug Administration.

Imagine the ease of a world where you could have Ambien Plus Bars for those sleepless nights. Parents would appreciate having Special Keflex Cereal on hand for those nasty ear infections that inevitably occur after office hours. Keep Xanax Fruit-Flavored Roll Ups in the candy dish in your office. Make the teacher happy and send junior off for a great day at school with a handful of Reece's Ritalin Pieces. Enjoy some guilt-free KFC Lipitor Hot Wings. Women could unsuspectingly slip their men Soft Batch Viagra Chip cookies.

Talk about a Happy Meal.

So I only had to deliberate for a moment. I delivered the verdict and my boys triumphantly threw the cereal formerly known as junk food into the cart. And who am I to argue? Because the day I see Premarin Pop-Tarts "Now with Botox!" you can bet I'm filling the cart.

Lessons on How to be a Mother-In-Law

I've known about her a long, long time. In fact, it's been over twenty years now. We know our respective roles. But she's out there. And I know it.

But The Husband is not off hiking an imaginary Appalachian Trail like Governor Sanford. He hasn't gone Arnold on me because he knows I would become The Terminator. He's never given me any reason to give his car the Tiger Woods treatment at 2 a.m. But there is another woman in The Husband's life – his mother.

Some people love nothing more than to share their very own Mother-In-Law-From-Hell story. A few out there have true tales that portray their own particular brand of Monster-In-Law as nothing short of a menopausal Lucifer with devil horns, a tail and dried up ovaries.

There's the rabid MIL-In-Training who tries, with the ferocity of a pit bull, to sabotage every relationship in her precious son's life. But sometimes love is not only blind, but mute and turns a deaf ear to the screeching warning siren known as his mother. By then the MIL has taken over the entire wedding in an attempt to turn it into a self-indulgent freak show. When MIL doesn't get her way her reactions range from the silent treatment to pouting and tantrums worthy of a two-year-old. In the name of preserving family harmony, the poor bride-to-be finds herself in a lacy, white Scarlett O'Hara hoop skirt looking like a cross between a *Gone With the Wind* extra and Little Bo Peep.

With the nuptials behind her, the naïve new bride believes that the wedding nightmare is over and MIL will now fade into holiday family gatherings where a few gin and tonics will at least put some fun into the dysfunctional.

But that is not to be. Because in the game of marriage, the MIL is just warming up. And she's about to go into a full court press of meddling.

MIL will now be content to offer her opinions on every issue of newlywed life, from where to open a checking account to how to properly iron a shirt. This will keep her occupied until the children come along. Because that's when the real fun begins.

And then the only time the bride will want to see her MIL is when she's in an urn.

So when someone who drew the short straw on MILs starts dishing about her very own Evil One, I'm all ears. I'm happy to offer empathetic encouragement to hear the worst of the dirt. But when she takes a breath and waits for me to chime in with ghastly tales of my own, I have to clam up. Because I can't say one bad thing about mine.

I'm a very lucky woman.

My MIL never uttered one word about our choice of nuptials. She's never said one syllable about the usual state of disarray of my house. Commentary on raising The Boys? Job well done, she tells us. She not only sends me Mother's Day cards, but thoughtful birthday and Christmas gifts as if I'm one of her own daughters.

Yeah, she's that good.

But my MIL has given me an even greater gift, one that she doesn't even know about: a lesson in how to be a mother-in-law. One day, in the distant future, I, too, will be a MIL. To my future daughters-in-law out there, let's just be clear on things right from the start. There will be no hoop skirts. Unless, of course, that's exactly what you want.

A Real Mother Meets the "F" Word

When you're pregnant, helpful members of the Sorority of Motherhood become your very own What To Expect resource guide. They function as a virtual Pregnancy Google, answering questions on the delightfully strange array of symptoms that accompany your changing body ranging from buzz saw snoring to ever-present flatulence. Once your little bundle arrives, they Sherpa you through that wild ride known as Baby's First Year.

Next thing you know your little darling is trotting off to kindergarten. By that time, the advice has dried up. And that's precisely when you could use some words of wisdom. But no one is talking. That's because they're trying to recruit you.

I'm going to spill the secret.

You're welcome.

Starting with kindergarten and continuing through your child's public school education, each and every year you are going to come face-to-face with the F-word.

I am talking, of course, about fundraisers. It seems I've been doing them most of my life.

When I was a kid, I walked door-to-door selling hot Krispy Kreme doughnuts every Saturday to raise money for our annual choir trip. They could have made even more money if they put me on the corner and let me sing – people would have happily donated to make me shut up.

What I lacked in vocal talent I made up for in enthusiasm.

I wasn't a good salesperson either, so my family ended up with enough chocolate bars in the basement that you'd expect Willy Wonka and a couple Oompa Loompas to answer our front door.

But it's that very enthusiasm that gets me in trouble now when it comes to fundraisers. No one warned me. In my world, it's the equivalent of Maternal Restless Arm Syndrome, like the Jimmy Leg, that is simply uncontrollable. And once again, I can feel myself raising my hand to volunteer for yet another project.

I am powerless to stop.

It's an out-of-body experience. I'm staring at my arm as it shoots up in the air while thinking *WHY AM I DOING THIS?* Again. But by the time my arm reaches full extension, I'm usually blurting out, "THAT'S A GREAT IDEA, I'LL DO IT!"

Gets me in trouble every time. Which is why I came precariously close to signing up to raffle a kidney for a new computer lab.

I've stayed up half the night trying to channel Buddy from *Cake Boss* in an effort to create the flawless fundraiser confection. What I usually end up with is a steaming mess in the garbage, a cake

Betty Crocker wouldn't claim and a bad case of Cake Envy on my way to buy cookies.

Bake sales are no piece of cake, people.

No matter what the task, I end up waving my arms like a Price Is Right Contestant at every fundraising committee meeting. Which explains my behavior at a recent High School Marching Band Uniform Fundraiser meeting. When someone suggested wearing a uniform while handing out fliers, before the words ever left her lips, my hand was in the air as I chanted, "THAT'S A GREAT IDEA, I'LL DO IT!"

I had a great time wearing it. And if there were super cute shoes involved, I'd still be marching around town in it.

So when someone suggests a committee member wear the uniform while dangling in the air above Main Street until we reach our goal, I know my brain will be saying "THAT'S NOT A GREAT IDEA! I'M AFRAID OF HEIGHTS!" but my arm will be flailing in the air anyway.

So honk and wave if you see me. Better yet, throw some money in the jar so they'll let me come down before spring.

Here Comes Trouble

I don't go looking for trouble. And abiding by that motto has served me well. But a few weeks ago, I had my first inkling of an interference with our familial karma early in the New Year.

Trouble was brewing.

Because little did I know on that Sunday afternoon at the gym when Younger Boy uttered those fateful words that he was ushering in The Bad Juju of 2012.

I just finished my workout when I spied Younger Boy rounding the corner still sweaty from his basketball game. I expected him to announce, "I'm hungry." Instead he said with an uncharacteristic degree of urgency, "Dad's hurt."

I found The Husband standing on one leg in the lobby. The injured leg, which he held off the floor, appeared to have a cantaloupe where his calf should be. "What happened?" I asked him. "We were playing basketball," he said. "He went down like he was shot," Younger Boy added helpfully.

The Husband vetoed my pleas to drive him to the Emergency Room. But I did manage to drive him crazy once I had access to WebMD where I searched Torn Calf Muscle. "It's a middle-age, recreational athlete injury, common in 30 to 50 year olds," I hollered so he could hear me in the other room. "But you're too old, do you think it's something else?"

He didn't answer.

"Did it give you a sharp pain in the back of your leg?" I asked even louder.

"Can you guess where you're giving me a sharp pain right now?" he answered.

Here comes trouble.

A couple days later, Older Boy called from his basketball game. "I broke my nose," he said. "I look like Bert from Sesame Street." When I picked him up to go the ER, he didn't look like Bert at all. He looked like Gonzo from the Muppets.

Trouble was knocking on my door.

On Sunday, Younger Boy sent me a text, "I think I hurt my ankle. BAD." Rushing home, we found Younger Boy's ankle the size of a watermelon. His foot appeared to be Photoshopped to his body at an angle not normally associated with a human hoof. A few hours later, the ER sent Younger Boy home in a cast and crutches.

Trouble was in the house. And I feared it was looking for me.

Friends told me not to worry because bad luck comes in threes. Apparently Trouble was unaware of this rule. Because just like Fraizer in the Thrilla in Manilla, Trouble wouldn't quit.

So it came as no surprise when the day of Older Boy's broken nose surgery dawned with a loud and vigorous chorus of wretching.

Trouble hadn't come for me after all. It came back for The Husband. And it brought him the stomach flu.

Trouble – 4. Team Testosterone – 0. I was the Last Woman Standing. I wanted to keep it that way.

So I decided to wear Younger Boy's sparring helmet, blanket myself in bubble wrap and sit in the corner of the basement with The Husband's 9 iron. Trouble might be looking for me, but I'd at least get in a few good licks first.

That night, as I observed the bruised and battered wreckage of my family - Older Boy with his post-surgery nose cast, Younger Boy's elevated ankle and crutches and The Husband with his head hovering over a bucket, I realized that Trouble would just have to wait. I had more important things to do.

Like take a picture – for our 2012 Christmas card.

Trouble's got nothing on me. But I'm keeping the 9 iron handy, just in case.

Scarred For Life

I was in the privacy of my own home. The shades were drawn. It was the middle of the day. There was no chance of getting caught.

Or so I thought.

In my haste, I overlooked one very important detail – locking the back door.

I don't know who was more startled. And I'm not sure exactly how much The Boys witnessed before I realized they were standing there. It was a scene no teenager should ever have to see.

The spectacle they observed was so utterly horrifying, so completely embarrassing for all of us that there is not enough therapy available to wipe that look of disgust off their faces.

There I was in my ratty Louisville sweatshirt, mismatched Smart Wool socks and Mom Jeans. And I was doing a Mid-Life Mom interpretation of Running Man all alone to a windowpane rattling volume of Party Rock Anthem.

I was totally busted – for bustin' a move.

Admittedly, my Party Rock shuffling lacked the youthful vigor of the dancers in the video or I would have ended up in a neck brace and traction. So my version looked more like Running Man meets Arthritic Amish Woman. But I didn't care because I was having a great time with Party Rock in the House as the dudes from LMFAO encouraged me to "shake that." And I was having so much fun I couldn't help myself. But I'm fairly certain the only way that the LMFAO fellas, or anyone else for that matter, wants to see me shake anything is through glasses with Vaseline smeared lenses.

Martha Graham once said dance is all about "discovery, discovery, discovery." But what I feared I would discover after The Boys observed my spastic efforts at self-expression was the two of them moving out in the middle of the night.

I like to dance. I'm just a little dance challenged.

There are bad dancers, like me, but let's face it - there are some really bad dances out there too. Some would argue that the list begins and ends with The Macarena. But what about The Hustle and YMCA? Anyone guilty of wearing Hammer Time parachute pants with the crotch hovering between your ankles and going all U Can't Touch This in your very own living room?

I thought so.

But even I, The Queen of Bad Dancers, am willing to admit a few of these goofy moves are fun to try in a group setting. It's hard to resist rocking the Chicken Dance or Cotton Eye Joe with my feisty granddad at a wedding reception. And after a couple gin and tonics, I start to think I look pretty good. At least until I'm forced to watch the video.

There's one dance (and song for that matter) that should be deemed a crime against humanity - Mullet Ray Cyrus' *Achy Breaky Heart*. In 1993, you couldn't go into any bar in Kentucky without hearing Billy Ray rhyme "gone" and "phone" just before being stampeded by a herd of Achy Breaky line dancers. It was enough to make you grab one of their Miller Lite bottles and attempt to bludgeon yourself into unconsciousness.

But one dance has always been and always will be beyond reproach – the Hokey Pokey. Don't say anything bad about it because I will put my whole self in and use my left foot to kick your butt.

So if my shades are drawn and Party Rock is in the House, don't come a knockin'. Because in my living room, I can be a Fly Girl. And Everyday I'm Shufflin' - in the privacy of my own home.

and now a word of thanks

The Husband, Older Boy and Younger Boy all deserve Big Hugs, and quite possibly therapy, for letting me hang all our family's laundry out there in my column. Because as they know all too well, it's the only laundry that stands a chance of getting done around here. These three merit a special thank you for living with me not only when I'm on deadline, but peri-menopausal.

Another round of hugs, as well as a round of shots, should go to The Parental Unit, The In-Laws and The Fam. Thanks for letting me tell these tales without threat of litigation. But should you get any ideas, I still have my Law School Get Out of Jail Free Card: The truth is an absolute defense. So there.

Buckets of chardonnay for my Real Mom Posse, who now footnote our conversations with "You're not going to write this, are you?" BFFs, thank you for always having my back. I owe you my most sincere thanks and quite possibly a kidney.

The Universe smiled upon me when I landed in this incredibly creative community in Montana. A Shout Out to this exceptionally generous and talented group of individuals whose kindness, advice and encouragement have helped me finally give birth to my new baby – this book. Thank you for making it the only pain-free delivery I've ever experienced.

And where would writers be without great editors?

A lifetime supply of red pens to editor and proofreader, Carla Little. Carla, thank you for your keen editorial eye and for never, ever letting my participles dangle.

A Big Thank You to Editor Megan Ault Regnerus who didn't laugh when I had the cojones to ask if I could write a column for *Balance Magazine*. Thankfully, she did laugh at my columns.

Heaps of Undying Gratitude to *Bozeman Daily Chronicle* Managing Editor extraordinaire, Nick Ehli. I'm especially thankful that the conversation about writing my column I *thought* I had with him while on crutches and Darvocet really happened. Thank you, Nick, for taking a chance on me and letting my tales of motherhood, relationships and middle-age find a home in the pages of the *Chronicle*. A job doesn't get much better than this.

But the biggest applause, fountains of champagne and dozens of big ol' red roses, goes to all the Mothers out there. It may take a village to raise our children but I think it takes an even bigger village of Real Mothers to keep each other sane in the process.

Thank you ladies, for Keepin' it Real.

About the Author

Denise Malloy lives with The Husband and The Boys in Bozeman, Montana. After working as a lifeguard, a Peace Corps Volunteer, a middle school teacher, a Hickory Farms girl who had to stand in front of the store dressed in tacky overalls and verbally assault unsuspecting passers-by with, "Would you like to try a sample of our beef stick?" a switchboard operator and finally, an attorney (but don't hold that against her), she is uniquely qualified to do absolutely nothing as evidenced by recent job interviews. That is why she writes.

Her columns appear in the *Bozeman Daily Chronicle*.

Visit her website at **www.denisemalloy.com**.

www.ingramcontent.com/pod-product-compliance
Lightning Source LLC
Chambersburg PA
CBHW060805050426
42449CB00008B/1546